*Conversations*

# Straight Talk
# with America's
# Sister President

# Conversations

## JOHNNETTA B. COLE

ANCHOR BOOKS
DOUBLEDAY
New York   London   Toronto   Sydney   Auckland

AN ANCHOR BOOK
PUBLISHED BY DOUBLEDAY
a division of Bantam Doubleday Dell Publishing Group, Inc.
1540 Broadway, New York, New York 10036

ANCHOR BOOKS, DOUBLEDAY, and the portrayal of an anchor are
trademarks of Doubleday, a division of Bantam Doubleday Dell
Publishing Group, Inc.

*Conversations* was originally published in hardcover by Doubleday in 1993.

Library of Congress Cataloging-in-Publication Data

Cole, Johnnetta B.
    Conversations : straight talk with America's sister president
Johnnetta B. Cole. — 1st Anchor Books ed.
        p.   cm.
    1. Afro-American women.  2. United States—Race
relations.
I. Title.
[E185.86.C5815   1994]
305.48′896073—dc20    93-27254
CIP

This one is especially for you, Sister Dr. Camille Cosby (and you, too, Dr. Bill), with love and gratitude for all that you have done for this Sister President

# Contents

# Acknowledgments

This book is intricately entangled with my sisters, an array of women with whom I share not a single connecting link of kinship but with whom I am undeniably bound by shared experiences and unmet dreams. And so, my sisters, this one is for you, about you, and most importantly because of you.

Because it is the truth, I can say to Tonya Bolden: "This book would not have been written without you." I wanted to talk with thousands of women, but there was little chance that I could do so without a truly skilled "operator." You have been just that, Tonya: from looking up unknown numbers and asking me once again, "How do you spell that name?", to eliciting from me substantive ideas that indeed allow me to communicate with my sisters, some of whom are nearby, most of whom are at a considerable long distance.

Tonya Bolden, the sisters with whom I am talking will not know, as you and I do, how very much you have contributed to this book. If they become engaged in this conversation and in any way benefit from it then they, like I, are forever in your debt.

For all of the jobs that an excellent literary agent does well, I thank you, Marie Dutton Brown. You have worked well with me because ultimately you and I work for the same goals.

Women at Doubleday have carefully and expertly handled my book and they have done so in a spirit of true sisterhood. I am grateful to you all, and most especially to Martha Levin. I am also indebted to Beverly Guy-Sheftall, my friend and colleague at Spelman who carefully read and commented on the manuscript.

I want to take this opportunity to thank all of the sisters whose very lives inspire my own. There are those who know this is so because our lives are linked in some way. There are others who I do not know personally, but to whom I feel close, perhaps because, as our old folks are fond of saying, "we must have been cut from the same piece of cloth."

I thank the 1,800 sisters who are the students of Spelman because so much of my work is with and for them, the alumnae of the college and those sisters who will come to this great women's school long into the future.

For their contributions to *Conversations,* I want to acknowledge four very special brothers. With extraordinary sensitivity and support my husband, Art Robinson, has been behind this project, as he is with all that I do. A good deal of how my sons—David, Aaron, and Ethan Che—and I have "raised" each other has found its way into this book. Thanks, sons.

Finally, I am indebted to an extensive network of my siblings, in-laws, stepsons, and other kinfolk; friends; and colleagues. My sisters and brothers all, thank you!

# By Way of Introduction...

INTRODUCTIONS ARE TRICKY. Usually, with only a few short minutes at our disposal we try to communicate the gist, the drift of a person, an idea. Of course, should the introduction drag on too long you can feel people urging you under their breath to: "Please, get to the point!"

In the interest of doing just that, let me say that I am writing this book because for too many African Americans things are not right.

"That is hardly news," you may well respond.

True, but things are getting worse.

Perhaps the most dramatic evidence centers on life and death. For the first time ever, life expectancy for African Americans is on a downward turn. There has always been a gap between Black and White life expectancy; but in the past, though we could never catch up, as White Americans began to live longer, so did we. Now, however, we are not expected to live as long as we used to. Quite simply, there are only two explanations: when we have poor health care, inferior education, wretched housing, and drugs in our neighborhoods, we are being destroyed; and when we in turn emotionally and physically brutalize our kinfolk, we are destroying ourselves.

No, things are definitely not right, not right for African American men, women, or children. No matter what the crisis, however, it is writ large in the lives of African American women, because it is we women who bring children into this world and serve as their primary caretakers. When African American women addicted to drugs have babies, this spells not only drug-addicted infants, but—barring outside intervention—neglected and abused children. If life circumstances and life choices leave us psychologically out of balance, most often our children will inherit that trauma. Just as with anger and frustration, if we let ignorance rule over careful and thoughtful ways, ignorance will usually also rule our children. Likewise, if we center our lives on BMWs, RVs, VCRs, PCs and the other acronyms of consumerism, we cannot expect our children to do otherwise.

We African American women must help cure whatever ails us, or more than likely, it will afflict those coming up behind us. And there is a danger that what now seems a light affliction may become a plague among succeeding generations, in which case the quality of life and life expectancy for African Americans may indeed sink to even lower depths. The phrase "The Children Are Our Future" should not be taken lightly or yawned at as a cliché.

If I thought only a few share my concern for our well-being and survival, I would abandon all hope for Black America. If I felt we are powerless to turn things around, I would lose all faith in African Americans. But I have hope and I have faith because I know that a great many of my sisters share my concern and have ideas on effecting change, on getting things—if not perfect—at least headed in the right direction. And so, I thought we would all do well to talk about the situation.

This is to say that this book is not intended as a monologue, nor do I wish to preach at African American women. I shudder at the thought that these pages might be perceived as a how-to book or a "Black Woman's Guide" to anything. Rather, it is intended as a dialogue. In a sense, it is also what you might call a multilogue because much of it emerges out of conversations I have had over the years with my extended family of grandmothers, mothers, aunts, sisters, and daughters; and I now invite you, my sisters, to join in the discussion.

Part I is a brief narrative of my world-view and some of the roads I have traveled personally and professionally. It is an attempt to share with you "where I'm coming from" literally and in terms of what I consider crucial issues in the lives of African American women, among them: racism, sexism, provincialism, self-help, and education. In Part II, I discuss these five subjects at greater length and one at a time—but with some overlapping. As you will see, in Part II no essay is an island.

This book is a conversation between me and my African American sisters, by whom I mean women of African descent who live in America. I have no objections to others listening in. If they do, then so much the better. For, while someone's eavesdropping can be disquieting, it may not be altogether such a bad thing. There are times when you are having a private conversation with someone and unbeknownst to you others are listening. Often the eavesdroppers will not only hear, but learn something. As a result, their thinking and behavior may be positively affected by what was, in fact, a conversation not particularly intended for them.

With that said, my sisters, let's talk!

*Conversations*

# "Will the Circle Be Unbroken?"

This chapter's title is taken from a song that assures the bereaved that death will not separate them from their dearly departed. The song has special significance for me because its imagery of the circle not only speaks to my life in ways that will become apparent later on, but also because it reminds me of the belief in African cosmology that we are all a part of the same circle: the living, the dead, and the yet unborn.

*To do your first works over means to reexamine everything. Go back to where you started, or as far back as you can, examine all of it, travel your road again and tell the truth about it. Sing or shout or testify or keep it to yourself: but* know whence you came.

    —JAMES BALDWIN, "The Price of the Ticket," *The Price of the Ticket: Collected Nonfiction, 1948–1985*

AUTOBIOGRAPHY is a potent and long-established facet of the African American literary tradition. If handled glibly and carelessly, autobiography simply becomes: "Let me tell you about my life." In the better tradition—Harriet A. Jacobs' *Incidents in the Life of a Slave Girl, The Autobiography of Malcolm X,* Maya Angelou's *I Know Why the Caged Bird Sings,* Pauli Murray's *Song in a Weary Throat, Assata* by Assata Shakur (born JoAnne Chesimard)—autobiography becomes a reflection of the realities of the lives of millions of African Americans: the realities of their oppression; the realities of their journey toward liberation and self-determination.

My life is certainly not a mirror image of that of all my sisters, and what follows is definitely not a full-fledged autobiography. A jaunt through my life will nonetheless, I trust, shed light on a host of issues that concern and confront African American women. I hope that it will also serve as a reminder that regardless of all the differences in our backgrounds and lifestyles there are ties that bind us together, connections that give us every reason to gather together in an a(wo)men corner, not only to testify, but to prophesy, too.

From Jacksonville, Florida, to Atlanta, Georgia, it is roughly a one-hour plane trip, 270 miles airport to airport. For me the distance between these two points was not short, nor was it a straight line. Yet my appointment to the presidency of Spelman College has been, I believe, a natural, even logical progression. Even though I never dreamed of becoming the president of Spelman (or any other college or university for that matter) my coming to that Black women's college has profoundly affirmed and reinforced my consciousness about race, gender, and class. This is to say that Spelman, as an institution and environment that promotes equality, justice, and human decency, has given me an opportunity to see and experience a touch of the ideal society for which I have struggled most of my life.

As an adult, the issues of race, gender, and class have been central in my life, my community activities, and my work as an anthropologist and teacher. The question that rests at the center of the work I have done, and continue to do is: How can people of color, women, and poor people become equal and productive members of their society?

Many times, particularly during the 1960s, I was accused of "seeing race under every tree." To which I responded: "That's because it's there." Coming into the 1970s, as I developed a feminist consciousness, I started seeing race *and* gender under trees. Furthermore, keenly aware that there are haves and have-nots in our society, I have been outspoken against the inequitable distribution of wealth, and hence power, that leaves a large percentage of our population shut out from the essentials of a decent life and locked into poverty and degradation. My sensibilities about these issues did not arise from a sudden dawning. Rather, they were by and large influenced and shaped by forces and circumstances beyond my control, primal among them, the time and people-scape into which I was born.

While class is a relative and often ambiguous term, it would be accurate to describe my beginnings as Black upper middle class. When it comes to class, one of its most visible signs are "things": what people own, what they have access to, what they covet. Growing up as a member of an upper-middle-class Southern Black family meant for me growing up with "good things"—art; classical music; fine china; and of course, books, from classics such as *Up from Slavery, Little Women,* and *The Iliad* to eclectic coffee-table books on the gardens of Rome, ancient architecture, and African art. At the same time that my mother taught me to recognize and appreciate what we often call "the better things in life," she also instilled the principle that I should never bow down to them. Mary Frances Lewis Betsch always put "things" in their proper place: after feelings and relationships.

Growing up in my particular family also meant that I grew up *known* in the community, because everyone knew my maternal great-grandfather, Abraham Lincoln Lewis. As the most prominent African American family in Jacksonville, the Lewises were not only for me, but for many people, bigger than life. The "colored" branch of the library was the A. L. Lewis Library; there was, and still is, an A. L. Lewis YWCA. I would be hard-pressed to say that the Lewises were totally immune from elitist attitudes often found among the well-known and well-to-do, but at the same time I can say that to a large extent they were able to keep it all in perspective. Proverbial pillars of the Mt. Olive African Methodist

Episcopal Church, the Lewises were a profoundly service-oriented family that took to heart the Biblical precept that to whom much is given, much shall be required.

This conviction was expressed by A. L. Lewis when in 1901 he cofounded the Afro-American Industrial and Benefit Association, "for the purposes of relieving the sick and providing for the respectable burial of the dead." This was at a time when White funeral homes would not touch a Black body and White insurance companies would not insure one. In response to those realities, my great-grandfather explained to me, he and six other men began the company to offer African Americans a reliable alternative to passing the plate on Sunday mornings every time a member of the congregation stood up and said, "We're sad to announce that sister Jenkins' husband has passed . . . could we help?" Years later as an anthropologist, I would understand that these men came together in the tradition of small West African economic cooperative arrangements such as the Sou Sou, where each member makes a weekly or monthly contribution to the communal pot and then, when he or she is in need, receives the whole pot. What those men began out of wisdom and creativity grew into the Afro-American Life Insurance Company, the first insurance company of any kind in Florida. The company eventually expanded beyond Florida into Alabama, Georgia, and Texas. Although the Afro, as it was known, went bankrupt in 1987, with the final holdings being bought by the Atlanta Life Insurance Company, folks in Jacksonville, Florida, still talk about how A. L. Lewis, the son of slaves, entered the work world

as a water boy for a Jacksonville sawmill and built
something for his family and his people.

Recognizing that African Americans could well appreciate opportunities for a better quality of life than
White America felt they deserved, in the 1930s my
great-grandfather developed the Lincoln Golf and
Country Club in Jacksonville and purchased beach-
front property on Amelia Island in Nassau County,
which grew into American Beach, the only beach
and resort community in the region then available to
African Americans. And while he himself only had a
sixth-grade education, A. L. Lewis knew the importance of education for African Americans and became a benefactor to Florida A. & M. University, Bethune-Cookman College, Florida Memorial College,
and other educational institutions.

Knowing A. L. Lewis—or "Fafa" as I called him as
a child—and his legacy could not help but shape my
consciousness. His altruistic and entrepreneurial
spirit taught me that we African Americans can and
must do for ourselves. This lesson reinforced principles I learned from my parents, who were industri-
ous and "race proud" and whom in retrospect I see
as proto-feminists. Like many people then and now,
in the ordinary course of living their lives my parents endorsed the idea of gender equality without
thought to the terminology or rhetoric in which people often get bogged down.

My father, John Thomas Betsch, Sr., was the only
child of a German brick mason and an African
American woman. I do not know much about his
beginnings, but I do know that from his birthplace
in Henderson, North Carolina, he found his way to
Washington, D.C., and Howard University.

In that circle that often characterizes our lives, I now live in Atlanta, the city where my mother and father first met. At the time, he was an agent for the Atlanta Life Insurance Company, and she had accompanied her family to an insurance meeting. Today, I serve on the board of the Herndon Foundation, which bears the name of one of my great-grandfather's contemporaries—another exemplary Black entrepreneur, Alonzo Herndon, the founder of the Atlanta Life Insurance Company.

My father eventually went to work for the Afro-American Life Insurance Company, but as he worked his way up through the ranks he always had his own enterprises on the side. For a while—and I am sure to the mild displeasure of the Lewises—he had a pool room and a little place called "The Waffle and Sandwich Shop" on Ashley Street, a commercial "colored street" much like 125th Street and Lenox Avenue in Harlem. My father was a warm, loving, caring man who was often called up in the middle of the night to get someone out of jail by posting his bond or vouching for his character. This strong, hard-working African American businessman was also not adverse to rolling up his sleeves in the kitchen and cooking, or taking my sister and me to buy shoes if it was more convenient for him to take us than it was for my mother.

My mother was one of the two children who survived of the nine born to Bertha and James Henry Lewis. There was never a question about college, she told me—of course she would go. After graduating from Wilberforce University in 1930, like many African American women of her generation and class, my mother became a teacher. In fact, my strongest early memories of a college professor is of my mom as a professor of English at Edward Waters College in Jacksonville, where she also worked as the registrar. Later my mother joined the insurance company her grandfather helped found, and she eventually rose to the position of Vice-President and Treasurer.

My parents never assumed that the success of the Lewis family would guarantee their own success. They had determined at the outset of their marriage that if they were ever going to make it, they could not become dependent on my mother's family. In the early years of their marriage they struggled to a certain extent, at times to the embarrassment of the Lewis clan. One of the famous family stories is of the day my great-grandfather came to our house on Louisiana Street and saw me and my sister playing with a ball made of rags. As the story goes he went straightaway to a store and bought us a "proper" ball. This episode as well as others I could cite reveal that while my parents did their best to make it on their own, the Lewises were there to smooth out the way if they hit any rough spots. As my parents plotted and pursued their course, they did some smoothing out for others, as well.

Like many African Americans of their generation, one very immediate way my parents reached out to others was in their embrace of what sociologists would later term the "extended family," but which in those days was considered "just being family," "just being neighborly," or just doing the right thing. When my mother was working at Edward Waters College she frequently brought home students who for various reasons could not go home for holiday breaks. One day in 1940 she brought home a student named Mildred Olivia Tucker, who never left. So in addition to my older sister and younger brother I also grew up with an "adopted" sister. From time to time other relatives and friends lived with us as different needs arose, and in this way, my parents gave me an experiential understanding of the varieties of Black families as well as what Black familyhood is like at its best.

Outside the family circle there were countless others who shaped the way I look at and move within the world. One was my first-grade teacher at College Park Elementary School, Ms. Bernice "Bunny" Vance (whom I then, of course, called "Mrs. Vance, Ma'am"). My closest childhood friend, BeBe Ross Coker and I still talk about the first day of class in the first grade when this small-statured African American woman made her way around that classroom of African American youngsters and asked each of us to give our names. I mumbled my name as best I could and then Ms. Vance, standing in front of me with the full force of her personhood, said, "Stand up, look me straight in the eye, and never again as long as you live mumble who you are." Ms. Vance was not the only person in my community who called for that kind of affirmation of self, but that encounter was a sharp reminder that being confident in projecting who one is is an important factor in how others will receive you.

Another important influence on my life was the legendary Mary McLeod Bethune. My great-grandfather was well-acquainted with Ms. Bethune, and among my mother's closest friends were a professor of romance languages and the librarian at Bethune-

Cookman College; and so, it is not surprising that as a youngster I knew the story of her founding the Daytona Normal and Industrial Institute for Girls in 1904 which later became Bethune-Cookman College. Early in my life Mary McLeod Bethune was pointed out to me as a woman I was to grow up to be like. I hasten to add that I know exactly who Mary McLeod Bethune was and I dare not compare myself with that great woman; but I do fully acknowledge my ongoing love of her and my debt to her as a pioneer in African American education. My admiration, of course, came with age. It would make great folklore to say that I remember receiving words of wisdom and my calling to education while sitting on the lap of Mary McLeod Bethune. But as a young girl what I remember most is being mesmerized by the wonderful hats she wore.

When I look back on my childhood I realize more so now than I did then, that from my immediate family and from members of the African American community in Jacksonville, I received strong messages about the worth and abilities of my people. I grew up feeling that "I *am* somebody" in the positive sense in which Jesse Jackson intended the phrase. Given my family background I had opportunities and advantages that many, many African American children did not. None of these positive aspects of my childhood, however, provided refuge from racism. Admittedly, my family's means and status did create some buffers. For example, as children we were driven everywhere to spare us from the humiliation of the back of the bus. Occasionally the laws of Jim Crow were temporarily suspended, as in the case of particular stores where a certain clerk who knew my mother, with advance notice, would arrange for us to have a private room in which to try on clothes. Of course, if I walked into any other store without my mother I could wait in line forever and certainly never be permitted to try on even a bracelet. Despite such cushioning I knew at an early age that there was, as is the case today, no amount of money or status that could shelter African Americans from racism in either its institutional or individual forms. This reality was poignantly expressed by Malcolm X in the question he once posed to a group of university students and faculty. As the story goes, Malcolm X asked, "What do you call a person who has a Ph.D. who is a Black American?" A very swift student responded: "Why, you call that person 'Doctor,' of course." "No," replied Malcolm X. "In America you call that person 'Nigger.'"

So there I was, raised in a financially comfortable, intellectually alive household, and yet my childhood memories, like so many other African Americans, are rife with classic insults and outrages: being called "Nigger" as early as the age of three; looking at the park across the street from our house at 1748 Jefferson Street on a dog-day afternoon and finding it hard to understand why I could not go into that swimming pool; traveling North with my parents and, as we moved through the Southern states at night, being terrified that the car would break down and the Ku Klux Klan would come. I will never forget the panic that stiffened my body the night we had a flat tire in a dark, isolated area outside of Jacksonville. As four White men approached us I knew what thousands of African Americans have known: the indescribable fear that they might be a lynch mob. To this day I remain certain that what kept us out of harm's way was my father's ability to make it known by some secret code that I could not decipher that he was a 32nd Degree Mason. Three of the men were, by chance, Masons, too.

I remember hating racism at the age of eight because "it" was what made my parents send me and my sister, Marvyne, to Washington, D.C., where African American children went to school for a full day. The Jacksonville school board had decided that half a day of school for African American children would save money—and besides, it was enough schooling for the "colored." I wanted to be at home with my Mom and Dad, and I knew that what prevented this was racism.

Alongside the memory of being separated from my parents, I remember my days in Washington with great affection. I remember playing hide-and-seek on clear, warm nights and Monopoly on rainy days with Art Robinson who lived with his Mom and Dad one door over from us. Thirty-five years later we would come together again in a second marriage for each of us. I remember how we would "be good" so that Mattye Betsch, my paternal grandmother with whom I lived, would let us get Popsicles from the Good Humor wagon. And I remember the night when my mother had come up for a visit and, as she soaped down my sister and me in the bathtub, told us that (at age forty-one) she would soon bring us a baby sister or brother. Some months later, John Thomas Betsch, Jr., came—the boy that Johnnetta was not! My father, beside himself with joy at having a son whom he assumed would follow in his footsteps as a businessman, went out and bought my mother every luxury present he could and could not afford. To the family's consternation, my brother followed his heart and his talents and became a jazz drummer. Today he lives outside of Paris and works mainly in Europe because like so many musicians he found that jazz—America's only indigenous music other than that of Native Americans—is largely unappreciated in its place of origin. Early on my brother let us know what was in store for him as he beat out rhythms on tabletops and any other surfaces he could get his hands on. While I was blessed with a passionate appreciation for music, John was musically gifted, as was my sister Marvyne.

Malcolm X's point about what an African American with a Ph.D. is called rings clear to me in the experiences of my sister. Marvyne attended Oberlin Conservatory of Music where she graduated with a double major in voice and piano. After further study in Paris, she moved to Germany where she performed leading roles in the German State Opera. But something happened to my sister in Europe. When she returned to America she began to display very erratic behavior, but her behavior was not so erratic that she could not talk about what it meant to be an African American woman living in Germany. She recalled, for example, occasions when members of the audience came backstage and exclaimed: *"Ach! Now it is clear why the Black one can sing Wagner. The name is Betsch!"* My sister's experience showed me that African Americans are victimized by the myth of White superiority at home *and* abroad, and that there are many ways to call us "Nigger."

Today my sister lives in Florida on the very beach developed by the insurance company my great-grandfather cofounded. Rejecting the material things in life, Marvyne, affectionately known as "the mayor of American Beach," dedicates her life to the preservation of that beach in its natural state. People don't usually associate environmentalism with African Americans, and particularly with African American women, but here is one who cares passionately about such issues as soil erosion, the destruction of the rain forests in Brazil, global warming, the potential extinction of various species of flora and fauna. She believes so strongly in the sanctity of nature that it is reflected in her way of life: her strict adherence to a macrobiotic diet, and her refusal to cut her hair or fingernails. When we were growing up neither of us could have predicted where the other would end up in life, but I do remember that when we were students at Boylan-Haven Marvyne and I agreed that the cooking classes that taught us to make cinnamon toast and hot chocolate were not the best preparation for whatever life held in store for us.

Boylan-Haven was where I received most of my secondary education. It was a private Methodist school for "Negro girls" where the teachers and administrators with one or two exceptions were White women. My sister and I were sent to Boylan-Haven because the "colored" schools in Jacksonville were so poorly funded. Attending Boylan-Haven meant we could be with our parents *and* get a "good education." By my sophomore year my parents finally gave in to my desire to go to Stanton, the only public high school for African Americans in Jacksonville. After one year there, at the age of fifteen, I entered Fisk University in Nashville, Tennessee. Like others who had appropriately pushy parents, I had been marched off to take an early entrance exam and then, having passed it, was sent on to college.

Fisk ushered me into the world of African American intellectuals on a level I had never known before. Prior to coming to Fisk I knew, of course, that James Weldon Johnson, who was born in Jacksonville, had written the Negro National Anthem. I had read W.E.B. Du Bois, Langston Hughes, and Claude McKay, among others and I knew quite well some of the arias that Marian Anderson sang. But to have, for example, almost daily contact with writer and critic Arna Bontemps who was the university's librarian, was awe-inspiring. My days at Fisk also gave me an opportunity to experience a vibrant collage of African American culture, from theatrical performances to art exhibits at the Fisk gallery to concerts by the Jubilee Singers.

While I was excited and nurtured by much of the life at Fisk, there was an aspect of the experience with which I had difficulty. For Fisk also meant that some "bougie" young women sat around boasting about their fathers' medical and legal practices, their mothers' fur coats, and speculating on which man they were going to marry from Meharry Medical College across the street. I was distinctly turned off by what seemed like endless discussions about money. I knew my family probably had as much if not more than those of some of these young women, but my mother had taught us that if you had it, you did not need to talk about it; and on the subject of marriage her position was that you did not need a man until you could take care of yourself.

In January 1953 my father died, and I was devastated by the loss. Hurt, confused, lonely, I decided to leave Fisk and transfer to Oberlin College. In retrospect, I was not running away from Fisk as much as from my father's death and toward my sister Marvyne who was then at Oberlin.

Oberlin was a culture shock, but in the end, an extraordinary intellectual experience for me. I was part of a little band of Black folk in a White sea. But it was a White sea that claimed to be a friendly one, and as one of the first American colleges to accept African American and women students, Oberlin quite justifiably maintained that it had been a friendly sea for many, many years.

Oberlin was a startling, intriguing adventure that showed me just how narrow and closed the South had been, where Black is Black and White is White. Oberlin was the antithesis of that. For the first time I had to distinguish among White people: they weren't all Southern and Christian! It was also my first real opportunity to interact with people from China, Hawaii, and various African countries. It was as if the world had come to me. At the same time, my experience was surely very much like that of many African American students at predominately White institutions today: fascination with and appreciation for other people, but homesickness for one's own. I began to feel that I had gone from one extreme to another. As much as I reveled in this diversity, there was a strong sense on my part that I did not have enough of my own folk around. How well I remember calling my mother one evening and telling her that I really didn't know what was wrong but sometimes I just missed being around lots of my people. My mother's suggestion was a simple one: namely, that I join a Black sorority in Cleveland since Oberlin did not have one. There was no need to ask my mother which sorority I should join. It was clear that it would be hers: Delta Sigma Theta Sorority. It took a lot of effort to travel forty miles to be a part of a Black sorority, but it was a trip well worth it. For a Southern young woman from a warm African American family and community struggling in the cold weather and overwhelmingly White atmosphere of Oberlin, Ohio, Delta Sigma Theta was a lifesaver.

When I entered Oberlin in the fall of 1953, I was still saying what I had said since childhood in response to "What do you want to be when you grow up?" "A pediatrician." In those days if you were female, being a doctor usually meant being a pediatrician. Surely you could not be a surgeon—only boys grew up to become that. But one class, "Introduction to Cultural Anthropology," permanently put to rest for me the idea of a career in medicine.

On the first day of class, Professor George Eaton Simpson stood before us and began to simulate hyperventilation, moving his body to Jamaican revivalist cult music. Between breaths he talked about this music, Jamaican religious cults, and much of the culture that is in the Caribbean and throughout the Americas as expressions of African culture in the New World. This, he said, is what anthropologists study. For me, it was an immediate, passionate reaction: Good-bye pediatrics!

Before my encounter with Simpson the word *anthropology* was not a part of my vocabulary. Once it was I enjoyed telling folks back home that I was going to be an anthropologist and waiting for the response, "Oh! What's *that*?!" I remember as if it were yesterday the day I announced to my grandfather,

"Papa, I want to be an anthropologist." My grandfather looked at me, and indeed responded, "What's *that*?!" I proceeded to describe what cultural anthropologists do and how they study people. My grandfather started laughing, told me point-blank that that was the craziest thing he'd ever heard of and added, "How in the world are you ever going to make a living doing something like that?" I burst into tears.

Alongside this vivid recollection of how my grandfather "crumpled mah feathers" as Zora Neale Hurston's Janie Crawford would say, stands the sweet memory that he later apologized and comforted me—but not without stressing that I'd better figure out how I was going to make a living. I also remember that my mother attempted to console me further and explain that my grandfather's reaction sprang from concern. She, too, stressed that I should not think that somebody would always take care of me, and that it was my responsibility to work *and* have a career. She then looked at me and said, "But if you do work that you hate, you will be miserable for the rest of your life. Find work that you love." She added, "If this is your passion, follow it."

Oberlin did not offer an anthropology major, but I took every course offered in the field, majored in sociology, and became Simpson's special student. With time and study my interest in anthropology only deepened, and the idea of becoming an anthropologist proved more than a passing fancy with a newfound, hundred-dollar word. As a result, there was no question but that I would go on to graduate school in anthropology, for the sake of a career and, ultimately, for my own well-being. I had some serious questions about being Black in America, and anthropology was at least speaking to, if not answering these questions. As I have often said to my students, you can either go through life haphazardly trying to respond to questions that trouble you, or in an organized way you can seek answers. I chose the latter. Granted, anthropology did not come with a set agenda that said, "Now, let me explain why it is that when you grew up in the South you had certain experiences," but it did give me the tools to better understand and gain some perspective on my experiences.

At the same time that I chose the field of cultural anthropology, I also knew my particular interest was Africa. This, combined with the fact that George Simpson had a close relationship with anthropologist Melville J. Herskovits meant there was only one place for me to go. I would study with Herskovits, the great scholar of African and African American culture at Northwestern where I would eventually earn my M.A. and Ph.D. in anthropology.

Herskovits had two special places in his heart: one for students who were African American, and another for students who were women. Both were in very short supply in those days, but there I was— both an African American and a woman. More importantly, however, I was a serious student, ready to be mentored. Years later as I continue to mentor young African American women anthropologists, I recall that when I was in college and graduate school I did not see myself reflected in the scholars who taught and encouraged me. I had to lean on the works of Zora Neale Hurston and St. Clair Drake to gain what all students surely profit from: evidence that if someone who looks like me has done it, surely so can I!

Herskovits was a pioneer in the study of African retentions in New World cultures. In *The Myth of the Negro Past,* published in 1941, he took an exceptional position. To this day I can remember first reading that book and gasping with shock and joy over what I learned there. Unlike the prevailing scholarship, he contended that Africans did not "prepare" themselves for the New World and slavery by stripping themselves of their culture; rather, they brought it with them. It was a culture that was then transformed and reinterpreted, but a culture that was, nevertheless, of Africa. You could see and hear it in the dominance of percussion in our music that echoes the centrality of the drum in African music; in the call and response in our worship services where a preacher's sermon is constantly punctuated with refrains from the congregation, just as in African ceremonies the leader calls out a phrase and the worshippers respond with the same or other words. African retentions in African American life can be seen and heard in the characters in our folklore where, for example, Brer Rabbit is a descendant of the trickster Anansi, the Spider of West Africa who is also found in African-based cultures in the Caribbean. And African retentions continue in the patterns of our families including the extended family and the matrifocal or mother-centered family. Herskovits further maintained that we continued to carry Africa in our language (okra, goober) and even in our body movements—the way we gesture, walk, and dance.

Today, for many this seems like old news; but forty

years ago such thinking was revolutionary—and even heretical, in the opinion of many. As it was for others, Herskovits' position proved a liberating insight for me. One, because it affirmed how terribly human we are. Just as Europeans had brought their cultures and ways of life to America, so too had Africans. The difference was not in who had and did not have a culture to bring on the voyage to the New World, but in what part of the ship one was placed for the long trip. At the same time, Herskovits' work gave me insight into how scholarship can contribute to the misrepresentation of a people. I came to see that the work of the Swedish economist and sociologist Gunnar Myrdal, and certainly that of sociologist and later New York Senator Daniel P. Moynihan, presented African American culture as a distorted, depraved version of White American culture. Such scholarship clearly misunderstood who we are as a people, fanned the flames of racial stereotypes, and in some ways contributed to our oppression.

A very important insight into another dimension of oppression came a few years later when I spent two years in Liberia, doing fieldwork for my doctorate in anthropology. The year was 1960, a time when the long-standing call for civil rights for African Americans began to take the form of the Black Liberation movement. Here I was in an African country, in a place where for the first time in my life I was in the majority. I was also in a country that was exceptionally intriguing because of its unique history: first as a place of resettlement in 1822 for freed slaves (Americo-Liberians), and then in 1847 as an independent country in which the Americo-Liberians set themselves up as an aristocracy and cast the indigenous people into a position of subservience.

Working in Liberia proved to be a pivotal experience, because it was there that I first really saw intraracial inequality. That is, I saw great economic, social, and political disparities between the Americo-Liberians and the indigenous people who shared the same basic color, hair type, and physical features. For the first time in my life I began to seriously consider the issue of oppression along class lines. It was an important discovery, particularly in the 1960s, when in America there was such a focus on oppression along racial lines.

The years I spent in Liberia also coincided with the first two years of my first marriage, and the birth of my first son, David. At Northwestern University I had met Robert Cole, a White American graduate student from Iowa. He was majoring in economics and, like me, was affiliated with the African studies program Herskovits directed. We were attracted to one another by shared intellectual and political interests which with time enabled us to cut through substantial differences in who we were and where we had come from. My mother was not enthusiastic about our relationship; his parents, even less so. With the reluctant approval of our parents, we went into the marriage with open eyes, knowing that an interracial marriage in America in the 1960s would bring down the wrath of White racists and Black nationalists. Within months after our marriage we went to Liberia, each to do fieldwork for our dissertations. There were wonderful and fruitful experiences during those two years in Liberia, and living in that kind of society certainly helped to cement an interracial relationship. We were outside America where Whites were in the majority numerically and in terms of power. We were in an African nation where Black folks were in charge. The marriage was a rich one in terms of an intellectual exchange. What ate away at the union was the more rapid advancement of my career as compared to his.

It had always been clear to both of us that I was going to pursue a career outside the home. When it came to our graduate work and the work within our household we functioned as a team. But underlying a marriage of equality on certain levels was a tension created by my success as an African American and a woman in a society where it is assumed that greater success is practically a birthright for White people and for men.

We returned to America in 1962 and settled at Washington State University in Pullman, Washington, where Robert took his first teaching post. Of course, I went along. Far more so than today, in those days women more readily and unquestionably went where their husbands found work. We both worked on our dissertations and shared the rearing of our son David. In 1966 our second son, Aaron, was born. I remember well those days of a toddler, an infant, *and* a dissertation. I, like most women, learned early on to put a child on one hip while stirring a pot, then turn down the pot, quiet and comfort the child, and return to some pressing problem of the moment. For some women the problem might be the trick of putting together a meal when time and resources are in short supply; for others, how to deal with a situation in her child's school. In my case those two problems were complicated by a third: the need to figure out how to write about some theoretical point in anthropology. As one of my colleagues puts it: Women are forced to be problem solvers, and we must do so in the face of constant interruptions!

I eventually became a professor of anthropology and later of Black Studies at Washington State University. Although Pullman, Washington, was a very isolated place, there was no place in America in the mid-1960s untouched by the anti-war and Black Liberation movements. As each was a critique in some fundamental way of American society—militarism on the one hand, racism on the other—they represented parallel thrusts for a more righteous America. Had they truly merged, each would have become more powerful; together, they would have more drastically and positively changed America than they did separately.

I would be hard-pressed to recount all the civil rights sit-ins and marches I'd participated in up to this point, but now that the cry for African American freedom was being heard along with a call for America's withdrawal from Vietnam, my protest activities increased significantly. In fact, Robert and I were such anti-war activists it could not help but spill out onto (and sometimes wear out) our son David, who on one occasion as we were leaving home for an anti-war demonstration made it quite clear that he did not want to go. We firmly but gently said, "Well, you are going to come with us," to which he responded, "I've got an idea. Why don't we get a big net and we could catch the war and then we wouldn't have to go and march anymore." This story captures my deep belief that who we are as individuals is powerfully influenced by what we have learned in our early years. Today, David Kamal Betsch Cole is a young jazz drummer and artist with a deep and abiding opposition to violence and militarism.

No matter the number of marches, sit-ins, and rallies I participated in, speeches I wrote and delivered, and petitions I signed, my activism for a more just and enlightened America at home and abroad was chiefly expressed in my work as an educator. At Washington State University, in the isolated wheat fields of Pullman, I struggled alongside African American students for a more progressive curriculum and cofounded one of the first Black Studies programs in the United States. Black Studies was the intellectual wing of a political movement—the Civil Rights movement of the 1960s. The absence of a political movement of that kind today may well explain why in some ways Black Studies is less forceful now than when it began.

Black Studies was never envisioned as a purely academic affair; it was always seen as an instrument in a larger process for liberation. We pioneered in asserting that there cannot be a wall between the community and the academy, and that to be a good student is ultimately to be a good teacher, just as to teach well is to be a lifelong student. Rejecting what Brazilian educator Paulo Freire called the banking method of teaching where professors make regular deposits of information into students' heads during the course and withdrawals during finals, my colleagues and I advocated an interactive mode of teaching and learning whereby students became

fuller participants in their education and empowerment.

My embrace of a different and more creative approach to teaching was not limited to the realm of
theory. I had to be creative in practice as well. In
those days we did not have the volume of information we now have on African American history and
culture. As a result, I was literally scrounging for
material to fill in the gaps in the small body of literature that then existed. Oftentimes, this meant turning to oral history, to living documentation. I would,
for example, give students the assignment of talking
with their parents and relatives about their lives and
reporting on what they had learned. For a course on
the Black Church my students and I would attend
Sunday services. When there was no textbook, we
began to write the textbook together.

As committed as Black Studies advocates were to
the concept of African Americans rediscovering ourselves as a people in the context of world history and
events, I think I speak for many of my colleagues
when I say that we were not as myopic as critics
made us out to be. We spoke out against what could
be called "White Studies" occupying front and center in American curricula while Black Studies was
"ghettoized" for minority students. Importantly, we
also spoke out against the reverse. The goal was a
balanced (and accurate!) curriculum that would include the studies of all people. Usage of the terms
"Eurocentric" and "Multicultural" was not as widespread as it is today, but criticism of the former and
the call for the latter was what progressive educators
and students were essentially about in the 1960s.

Today, there are still misperceptions about Black

Studies and unfortunately its presence in college and university curricula is once again being challenged. Ironically, Black Studies at historically Black colleges and universities is rarely well-developed. Faculty and administrators at these institutions often argue that they do not need Black Studies because the majority of the student body is African American, and so is a good percentage of the faculty and staff. This line of reasoning misunderstands the nature and the role of this interdisciplinary field. Black Studies is not simply some automatic understanding that flows from being Black, but a conscious inquiry into the history, culture, and sociopolitical condition of African and African American people. And, it is an exploration that calls for understanding African and African American realities *in* the world, not divorced from it.

In 1970 I joined the W.E.B. Du Bois Department of Afro-American Studies at the University of Massachusetts at Amherst. What an entrance we made into Amherst: Robert and I had an eight-year-old, a four-year-old, and a baby on the way, plus two Russian wolfhounds! A few months later, Ethan Che Cole was born; two weeks later, I was back in the classroom.

I came to the University of Massachusetts in Amherst to work in the area of Black Studies and anthropology, but soon I found myself developing a greater awareness of sexism and an interest in Women's Studies. Like the majority of African American women of my generation I had come to a consciousness about sexism rather late in life. Growing up in the South I was intensely aware of race and racism, but my consciousness of gender prejudice was far less developed. Sure, I remember getting furious any time someone told me, "Girls don't do that." (Want to get me to climb a tree? Tell me girls don't do that.) And during my reign as double-dutch champion I had no qualms about making the boys turn rope. I had that speck of consciousness, but I didn't think about gender issues much beyond that.

I was not alone in coming to a consciousness about gender inequality at this particular time. In the 1970s many American women gave voice to their oppression and discovered power in joining with other women against it. The arena of my exploration and protest against gender inequality was primarily academia where the women's movement gave birth to its intellectual wing, Women's Studies.

As my interests in Black and Women's Studies merged, one of the earliest and most painful realizations I had was that in Black Studies it was hard to find women, and in Women's Studies it was hard to find Black folk. How could an interdisciplinary field dedicated to understanding one kind of oppression not have a sensitivity to another? But it happened. Black Studies did not insist that the accomplishments and experiences of African American women infuse the Black Studies curriculum on a par with those of African American men. Similarly, Women's Studies failed to adequately address the particular issues of African American women, not to mention those of other women of color, Jewish women, lesbians, the elderly, and women who are poor or disabled. The ability of intellectuals to engage in criticism and self-criticism and to "change their minds" is reflected in the fact that today, Women's Studies gives greater attention to the realities of diverse women; and within Black Studies, *her*story is no longer totally eclipsed by *his*tory.

Two years after coming to Amherst, I took my first trip to Cuba. Intellectually that trip was the first step in closing the Pan-African circle that I began to draw as a graduate student. My master's thesis had been on an African American church on the South Side of Chicago. The fieldwork for my doctorate had been conducted in Liberia. As years passed I increasingly focused my attention on the Caribbean, eventually carrying out studies in Haiti, the Dominican Republic, St. Croix, and Grenada. Despite the prevailing view that Cuba was a strange Communist country disconnected from other neighboring nations, I discovered that it was profoundly Caribbean—Afro-Caribbean, at that. Following my initial trip in 1972, I went to Cuba many times and during a sabbatical from the University of Massachusetts, I carried out fieldwork there on the issues of race and racism. I looked to Cuba for evidence that racism and sexism really are not genetic, that they are not systems which individuals biologically inherit and then express in every society in the world. What I found was a society that had not eliminated discrimination based on race and gender. But in an intriguing and significant way, Cuba is a place where there is less racism, but more sexism than in my own country. Today Cuba is a very different place than it was when I first visited there twenty years ago. The movement of the former Soviet Union and other Eastern European countries toward "Western" economic and political models and Cuba's refusal to do so has isolated that Afro-Caribbean nation not only from the United States, but from many other countries as well. One has to wonder what effect such isolation will have on the progress Cuba had been making toward eliminating racial and gender discrimination, and the definitive ways in which the Cuban form of socialism has provided more equitable access to health care, housing, education, and the arts than in any other Latin American or Caribbean nation.

In 1982 my academic journey took me from the University of Massachusetts to Hunter College as a Russell Sage Visiting Professor in Anthropology. That was also the year of my divorce, ending a twenty-two-year marriage. In the mixture of excitement and healing that follows the painful experience of divorce, I discovered the joys of New York City and grew closer to my three sons. I watched them, smart and lively youngsters of biracial parents, continue the ongoing struggle about their identity. Living in a lovely but much too expensive apartment not far from the large Black and Puerto Rican project called Red Hook, and struggling and succeeding in a Brooklyn public high school helped my youngest son Ethan Che to comfortably see and like himself as an African American. Now as a student at Morehouse, Ethan Che exemplifies the saying that a person must be at home somewhere before he or she can be at home everywhere.

Aaron, the middle son, delighted us all with his deep-seated interest in Japanese language and culture. During his junior year at New York University, he lived with a host family for eighteen months in Osaka, Japan, and this quiet and rather shy young African American man began a serious study that today finds him with an impressive command of the

Japanese language. Working now in Fukuoka, Japan, Aaron talks of graduate studies in Japanese language and politics. And to the question, why is a young Black man interested in Japan, why not Africa?, Aaron responds in the spirit of Zora Neale Hurston: "The world is my oyster. . . ."

David completed his major in fine arts at Williams College and announced that drawing, painting, and printmaking would always be a part of his life, but jazz is the more central passion. I recalled my mother's support of my passion for anthropology, my own love of jazz, and offered every support that I could as he began the long and serious process of becoming a jazz musician. As I watch David exercise the discipline and hard work that will take him to his dream, I hear the words of our sister artist Lorraine Hansberry: ". . . though it be a thrilling and marvelous thing to be merely young and gifted in such times, it is doubly so, doubly dynamic—to be young, gifted *and black*."[1]

During this period at Hunter College I taught some of the most creative courses of my career. In my course, "Introduction to Cultural Anthropology," I sometimes assigned students a visit to Bloomingdale's and an essay on what they had learned from this visit about race, gender, and class in American society. At other times, an assignment called for a bus ride from Hunter College on the east side of the city up to Harlem and a report on what that voyage taught students. During this period I also edited two anthologies, *Anthropology for the Eighties*

[1] *To Be Young, Gifted and Black: Lorraine Hansberry in Her Own Words,* adapted by Robert Nemiroff (Englewood Cliffs, N.J.: Prentice-Hall, 1969).

and *All American Women: Lines that Divide, Ties that Bind*, and I had brief and very positive visiting professorships at Williams College and at my alma mater, Oberlin College. Like many, I found the best therapy in the world is work. Lots of it!

In 1986, shortly before the search began for the president of Spelman, I was quite happy with my life in New York and at Hunter where by that time I was also the Director of the Latin American and Caribbean Studies program. Feeling strongly that I needed to be in the field, I was ready for a new research project. An anthropologist who isn't in the field periodically is like a concert pianist who performs but rarely practices.

It had always struck me as odd that American anthropologists had never really confronted our own society. I decided that I would, and began thinking of a megaresearch project on American society that would cut across racial, ethnic, and socioeconomic lines. I planned to approach a foundation for the substantial monies required to finance a team of American anthropologists who would simultaneously work in urban and rural communities across America—a Black farming community in Mississippi, a White farm town in Iowa, an Asian community in California, an enclave of the elite in New York's Westchester County, a Mormon community in Utah, a fishing village in New England, a Puerto Rican community in New York City. These anthropologists would pose the same kinds of questions about mores and traditions they would pose were they in Jamaica, Peru, Samoa, Thailand, or Zimbabwe. The compilation of their findings, I hoped, would result in a major tome that would expose the extraordinary diversity of American life and explain what in the world is American culture. It was during the time I was conjuring up visions of this enormous undertaking that I had one of the most spiritual experiences of my life.

In July of 1986 I led a group of thirty-one students and several professors from the City University of New York to Brazil for a seminar held at the Pontifical Catholic University in São Paulo where we explored central themes such as slavery and the role of women in the lives of African people in the United States and Brazil. The seminar was fascinating, and second only to the experience of being in the country with the largest population outside Africa of people of African descent, a place that pulsated with African culture, from the smells of the food being cooked on the streets of Bahia to the sounds of music in Rio de Janeiro.

At the conclusion of the seminar, one of my Brazilian colleagues asked if I would like to go for a divination. With my anthropological appetite duly whetted I responded, "Why, of course I would!" Immediately I began to wonder how this experience would compare and contrast with divinations I had witnessed years earlier in West Africa.

On a Saturday morning we drove to a working-class neighborhood in São Paulo and pulled up in front of a modest-looking house. Inside, we found the living room filled with women, all waiting to find out what the diviner could tell them about their futures. Because I was a guest in their country, the women decided that I should go first. After I was introduced to the diviner, Maruca, and she had agreed to see me, I followed her into her bedroom. She sat at the end of her double bed, I, at a table facing her, and to the left of the bed on a trunk sat a friend who would translate from Portuguese into Spanish, a language I could understand.

"This is the stuff of anthropology!" I thought as I looked down at the table and saw familiar items, things which are used in West African people's divination: a glass of water to entice the water spirit and a pile of cowrie shells which enable the diviner to look into the future. And there too was a wooden clenched fist, found all over Brazil to ward off the evil eye. With great anticipation I looked up at Maruca and met with a piercing gaze. "State your name," she said. And I did. She grabbed the cowrie shells, but as she was about to throw them in order to read the particular pattern in which they fell on the table, she went into what I could only assume was a trance.

The first thing Maruca said to me was "You will shortly change your job." "Well," I thought, "this is interesting, but I am very happy at Hunter College." She went on to say, "You will soon do what few women in your country do. It is a job done by men. And what you will do will be extremely important for our people." Here, she ran her index finger across the back of her hand to indicate that she meant Black people.

"There will be some people who will not want you to be there," Maruca continued. "But if you remain in touch with your Orishas, your spirits, all will go well." She then went on to tell me some other things about my past and my future, including the fact that I would remarry—which, like leaving Hunter, was the last thing on my mind. Maruca also told me of seeing the long line of my ancestors, back to a place in West Africa. She told me that I was a woman of exceptional strength who had come from people of unusual strength. I left Maruca's house shaken and perplexed, not quite sure how to "process" the experience. Because I had received Maruca's words in a translation from Portuguese to Spanish, could it be that I had misunderstood her messages? No, I learned through experience. I had understood quite clearly.

Call it prophecy; call it coincidence, but when I returned to my office at Hunter College in August, the first thing that caught my eye was a note from Donna Shalala, then president of Hunter, which read, "Call me about Spelman College." There were messages from other colleagues as well, and when I returned their calls I found that many of them had also telephoned to tell me that the presidency of Spelman was open and urge me to apply.

During the course of my years at Hunter I received more than a few letters and phone calls asking me to consider being a candidate for the presidency of such-and-such college or university. As a matter of fact, I had received several such inquiries before the Spelman search began. Naturally these inquiries gave me pause to toy with the idea, albeit fleetingly, of changing my career path, but I did not think of myself as a college or university president.

When it came to Spelman, however, I toyed with the idea more seriously. After I applied there came instant doubts. For one, I had not gone through the usual steps of the academic ladder that lead to a college presidency: chair of a department, dean, and vice-president. Second, although I had never visited Spelman, I was aware of its reputation as a conservative, "high-sedity" institution for "high-yellow" women, or as they were called, "girls."

How would I fare in such a place as this? I no less wondered how such a place would find a fit with someone like myself who was not only a single but a divorced woman, someone who comfortably described herself as a feminist, someone who had intellectually explored how different societies are organized—from the so-called primitive communism of traditional African societies to modern-day Cuban socialism. How would the Spelman community accept someone who was associated politically with progressive ideas, and who had a perspective which was then usually called "Black consciousness" and which today is more often referred to as "Afrocentric"? I remain respectful of and grateful to the women and men of Spelman's Board of Trustees who fully explored who I am and went on to support my candidacy.

After the short list of candidates had been determined, as were the other remaining candidates, I was brought down to visit Spelman and meet with the faculty, with staff, and with the students. For the most part all went well, but at one point I almost guaranteed that I would not become Spelman's seventh president.

During the course of a meeting with the faculty, one professor asked, "Dr. Cole, what has been your experience as a fund-raiser? What can we expect from you?" Drawing on nothing but sheer honesty I replied, "Well, I have certainly raised funds as a faculty member, but I have to say that in the sense in which you mean fund-raising, I have never raised a dime. But," I added, "I think I am capable of raising millions." Two years later, and ironically in that same room, another faculty member reminded me that when I had said I had never been a major fund-raiser that put the Spelman faculty in a most nervous state of mind. She went on to say, "Little did we know then that at your inauguration a gift of $20 million from Bill and Camille Cosby would be announced." Today, several years since Dr. Bill and Sister Camille, as I affectionately call them, gave Spelman the largest gift a family has ever given an historically Black college or university, I still pinch myself to believe it.

When my appointment was made it was clearly an historic moment for Spelman College and as I moved across the country speaking as Spelman's "Sister President," I came to see that this appointment belonged to all Black women. This school which originated in 1881 as the Atlanta Female Seminary in the basement of Friendship Baptist Church for the express purpose of educating African American women had been led by four White women and two African American men. There had never been an African American woman president of this African American women's college. For years Spelman students, faculty, and alumnae had been calling for a president who reflected the student body. Indeed, one doesn't have to work all that hard to see the deferment of this dream as a metaphor for the history of African American women, and their struggle against racism and sexism.

After my appointment several friends from around the country sent me a pair of white gloves, a joke that spun off of the fact that much earlier in Spelman's history the students as well as the women faculty and staff put on white gloves whenever they went to town. But times have clearly changed at Spelman, and I have never once had occasion even to consider wearing a pair of those gloves. For the Spelman I came to was far more traditional than conservative, which is to say that there is an appreciation for traditions as opposed to diehard opposition to any form of change even at the cost of stagnation. While there are, as there has always been, a number of students who come from very well-heeled families, over 80 percent of the student body receives financial aid, most of which is need-based. And a stroll through a series of yearbooks or a walk around the campus will show that Spelman students have always been as diverse in their skin tones as they have been in their academic interests.

Although I did not find a strong, vibrant African American Studies program, nor a fully developed major in Women's Studies, there was a vitality and dynamism about Spelman that didn't make it difficult for me to see Spelman's potential for becoming a renowned center of scholarship on women of Africa and the African diaspora. This course upon which I see Spelman embarking will entail new ways of approaching Africana and Afra-American studies, much as the course I am now on involves new ways of thinking, new ways of behavior.

I am deeply aware that I am a part of new ways of thinking and functioning because, although my situation is not unique, it is a far cry from the norm. When I give and get hugs from Spelman students, when they openly share with me their dilemmas and

their delights, I am aware that such a familial relationship between a college president and students is
not conventional. Similarly, it is not typical for an
African American woman to head an institution that
has name recognition in a society that still has the
attitude that men, and particularly White men, must
run an institution if it is going to be run well. I am
less intrigued by the fact that I am one of the exceptions to the "rule" than I am with its implication for
approaches to leadership. While I don't sit and ponder, "How do I as an African American woman ad-
minister this college?", I am aware that my sensibilities borne of my experiences as an African American
and a woman prompt me to "run things" in a manner that is not only efficient but much more humane
than the top-down dictatorial style of management
found in many institutions. I likewise feel myself
something of an explorer into new and different
ways of seeing and doing things in an area much
closer to home. For when I entered into my second
marriage, here, too, I found myself in an uncommon situation.

I still recall the day I returned Arthur J. Robinson,
Jr.'s phone call and realized within minutes that although we had not seen each other in thirty-five
years I was talking with my buddy, the person I was
almost inseparable from when we lived one door
apart from each other in Washington, D.C. I remember the exchange that followed his question,
"Tell me, do you still like jazz?" "How could you ask
such a question," I responded, "don't you remember when we were seventeen and you visited me in
Jacksonville, *I'm* the one who introduced *you* to jazz."
"That's true," he said, "you helped me buy my first

jazz record." "Well," I followed up, "I'm going to New York in a couple of weeks to hear some jazz at Sweet Basil." Before I could extend an invitation, he asked, "May I join you?" He did.

Our relationship was on the one hand much like traveling a familiar road, but on the other hand, when we married in 1988 we entered into largely uncharted territory. What does it mean for a college to have a "First Man" as opposed to a "First Lady." And, indeed, what does it mean for our marriage?

There is a sense in which coming to Spelman is more than a return to where I've come from. It is a reconnecting with my beginnings and the most fundamental part of who I am. This reconnecting has been expressed in simple things such as eating more collard greens (with, I might add, the challenge of preparing them or having them prepared without fatback) to matters far more significant such as rediscovering the importance of the Black Church not only as our Town Hall, but also as the historical venue where we African Americans express the deep and abiding spirituality our forebears brought with them to America. Coming to Spelman has meant interacting with women and men who remind me of the relatives, teachers, ministers, librarians, and YWCA directors in Jacksonville who played such positive roles in my development.

As I was packing up to move to Atlanta, my middle son, Aaron, taunted me with: "Twenty-one days until you move to the South! . . . Nineteen days before you move to the South!" and so on. I would always respond, "I'm not going to the *South*. I'm going to Atlanta."

To my mind, Atlanta represented the New South, a place far, far different from the South in which I grew up. This is not to say that racist attitudes (not to mention actions) no longer exist in Atlanta. For example, I am aware that in the minds of many, Spelman is perceived as "that little colored girls' school over there in the southwest part of town," and that I am seen yes, as a college president, but as president of "one of those *Black* schools." Still in all, coming to Atlanta has meant coming to a better, if not an ideal, South. Of course, vestiges of the Old South are all the more muted in my life because I spend so much of my time in a place such as Spelman.

I would prefer not to describe an experience in terms of the absence of something else, but I cannot avoid it when it comes to describing what it is like to be at Spelman. The absence of persistent and blatant racism and sexism on our campus is not only joyous, it is exhilarating. Sometimes when I am not quite sure why it is that I am fundamentally so happy here, even when there are wrinkles in my day and setbacks that come with the territory of being a college president (and a human being), I realize that in large part the explanation lies in the fact that far more than at any other time in my life in the United States, I live without racism and sexism defining each and every one of my actions, thoughts, reflexes, and defenses. In some sense it is a model of what our nation might be like because the Spelman family is not without men, nor is it composed exclusively of African Americans; and Spelman is a place where African Americans and all others have the freedom, the encouragement, and the responsibility to reach their potential.

To acknowledge that Spelman is a gender- and racially mixed environment is not to minimize the fact that it is an historically Black college for women. When I was a student at Boylan-Haven had anyone asked me how I felt about going to an all girls' school, I don't know how I would have responded, other than, perhaps, with a shrug and a "It's okay, I guess." Over forty years later, however, I am very conscious and proud that I am at an African American women's institution and moreover one where two-thirds of the faculty are women and three-quarters are African Americans. And I see the positive effect it has on the students. A student does not enter a classroom braced to battle the assumption that she cannot and will not excel solely because she is an African American and a woman; nor when she does excel does she have to swallow or rail against the left-handed compliment that she is somehow different from other Black folk, an exception to the rule. Instead, she can devote her energies to the business of learning and achieving. Moreover, this student does not have to wonder about her possibilities for achieving because someone like her who has achieved is standing before her or not far away in the position of professor, department chair, dean, provost, and president. This is what role modeling is in its ultimate and most penetrating expression.

While coming to Spelman and Atlanta was much like coming home, it was certainly not a private affair. The prominence I knew in Jacksonville, Florida, and the recognition I received within academia for my work in the area of cross-cultural studies of race, gender, and class was nothing compared to what I would meet after my appointment to Spelman.

The media attention I received as Spelman's first "Sister President" was phenomenal. And I'll never forget the Saturday morning my youngest son, Ethan Che, called me up while I was on a fund-raising trip for Spelman to tell me excitedly that my name had appeared on the "Soul Train Scramble Board." He was impressed: his mom the educator and intellectual was being projected in a forum of popular culture.

On the heels of all the publicity came invitation after invitation for speaking engagements, numerous awards, and a host of honorary degrees. Much to my amazement, at various functions, and even at airports, people were asking for my autograph. Before long I was being projected as a national leader in American higher education. The attention was very satisfying because it helped bring Spelman and by extension all historically Black colleges and universities into the national consciousness as vital and significant institutions. At the same time the publicity was unsettling. For one, I knew that should something go awry, the media would in all likelihood be no less "on the case." Moreover, I could see at work the familiar scenario whereby the establishment singles out one or two individuals as the voice of all of Black America. Clearly, I and any other single individual should not be and could not be *the* spokesperson for historically Black colleges and universities or *the* spokesperson for African American women. Then, too, there are the little discomforts that come with being a public figure. For example, one evening I was at home in the President's house at Spelman in a pair of jeans and a sweatshirt that read: "Proud to be Black, Beautiful, and Brilliant." In a sudden dash to the supermarket I stopped inside my door and wondered, "Should the president of Spelman be seen in this particular sweatshirt? Should she even be seen in the local A & P in jeans and a sweatshirt at all?" Fortunately, I don't take myself so seriously as to think that Spelman or the state of American higher education will rise or fall based on what I wear. I kept on the sweatshirt and jeans, put on and zipped a jacket up all the way, and as we say, I try to "keep on steppin'."

One of the most positive consequences of being a public figure is that it has given me an opportunity to interact and talk with more African American women than ever before. It is not as if I go around "studying" you, my sisters, but there is a sense in which my sphere of inquiry into the conditions and concerns of African American women has dramatically expanded. At large functions and small gatherings, whether it is a speaking engagement at a church on Women's Day or a meeting of my Literary Club in Atlanta, the National Board of the Coalition of 100 Black Women in New York, or the Spelman College Corporate Women's Roundtable, I hear certain notes repeated over and over again.

On the one hand there is a note of fierce pride in the strides African American women have made in the arts, business, education, politics, science and technology, and other arenas. There is a yearning and an expectancy for still greater achievements. I also hear a very positive sense of self and a rejoicing in being an African American woman. One of the most visible signs of this spirit is in the growing number of African American women wearing naturals or braids, or who incorporate more and more African elements such as *kente* cloth into their wardrobes and into their work and home environments.

At the same time, I hear undertones of despair over aspects of the personal and professional lives of African American women, and the life of their community. One of the strains I hear is of a certain loneliness and a longing for an intimate and supportive relationship that will enhance as opposed to define and stifle their lives. Another is of profound frustration and anger over the persistence of racism and sexism in the workplace. I hear this from women in entry-level and middle-management positions, and particularly from those closest to the top of the corporate ladder—high-powered, superbly trained, top-level executives who are saying, "Because I am Black and a woman I *still* have to go to this highfalutin job day after day and prove that I am a person of value. . . . This is not the way I want to spend the rest of my life."

In social and professional settings alike, as I join in discussions with African American women on the crises that confront our people, one of the most painful admissions I hear is, as one woman put it, "I am afraid of my own people." This woman went on to recount an evening when she was walking down the street and saw an African American man headed in her direction and she panicked. With tears welling up in her eyes she went on to describe the agony and shame she felt the moment her eyes met his and she knew that he knew that she was afraid of him and he intended her no harm.

And so, alongside melodies that affirm African American womanhood, I hear strains of despair. And it is not uncommon to find that it is one and the same woman singing both tunes.

Now that I am a college president, living in a large house, with a car and driver at my disposal, and VIPs in my Rolodex, I've sensed some people wondering, "How can she really be in touch with the day-to-day desperation and life-and-death sufferings of our people?" If life has taught me anything, it is that you do not have to be planted in the middle of abject poverty to know that distress is all around you.

Indeed, as the President of Spelman and board member of various institutions, organizations, and corporations, I have come to travel in circles in which I have never traveled before. As a result I often think of poverty in juxtaposition to wealth in a way that I never have before in my life. When I attend meetings in lavishly appointed corporate offices, I can't help but think that the furnishings cost more than many people will earn in a year, and more than others will ever have as disposable income.

I also see despair in juxtaposition to hope more keenly than ever before. Spelman may not be a paradise, but it is an environment where individuals are encouraged and empowered to be a positive "somebody" in their walk through life. When I leave the campus I am all the more aware of the discouragement and powerlessness that marks the lives of so many African Americans in the area surrounding Spelman. When I drive a few blocks from the campus past a church that runs a soup kitchen and see

African American men lined up at the church's door, I am conscious that there stand twenty, thirty, forty individuals who may be written off by society as nobodies. The presence of these African American men on a soup line inevitably makes me think that there also stand twenty, thirty, forty fewer brothers participating with sisters in a co-nurturing, co-socializing role as fathers, brothers, uncles, or friends to African American children.

There are occasions when I do not have to use the powers of deductive reasoning nor those of human empathy to know the suffering of another. Those aware of my commitment to community service and Spelman's often approach me about opportunities for students to put hands and feet to their words. Such was the case with a pediatrician from a local public hospital. As I toured the special child care unit, I saw incubator after incubator of human life weighing less than a pound: babies born to crack-addicted mothers. I wondered, indeed, what can Spelman do? That our Director of Community Service followed through on our visit and found Spelman students willing to spend time at that hospital rocking some of those babies, to a certain extent relieved the anguish I felt. But the image of those babies lingers still. It serves as a constant reminder that in cities all across this nation there are babies who need rocking, babies whose mothers need some rocking, too.

This is, of course, neither the time nor place for me to ponder what the future might hold for me in terms of my life's work. I know that my immediate task at hand is to do my part in assisting Spelman in becoming all that it can be. And while I would like to think that the mega-research project I dreamed of in 1986 is not on eternal hold, I cannot speculate much beyond this. All I know is that I hope to continue to explore and expose ways in which African American women and others can one day be full and productive members of this society. Beyond this, only time and no doubt forces greater than I will tell.

Some years ago I came across T. S. Eliot's poem "Little Gidding" and the famed lines: "We shall not cease from exploration/ And the end of all our exploring/ Will be to arrive where we started/ And know the place for the first time." These words have greater significance for me now than they did then, for in many respects I have indeed come full circle, and the points to which I have returned I see in new and different ways. While I still contend that racism and sexism are fundamental problems in American society, I no longer see race and gender under every tree—only under every other tree. Moreover, I now see more clearly that if asked to pledge my allegiance first and foremost to either the African American struggle for liberation or the women's movement for liberation, I would be unable to choose. How could I carve myself in two? For I know that my sisters and I, to borrow from Anna Julia Cooper, bear the combined "weight and the fret of the 'long dull pain'" of racism and sexism. And having one pain removed without the other is not to be free of pain. Finally, I know as if for the first time that although the ideologies of racism and sexism are to a great degree inherited, they are not genetic, which is to say that just as they have been learned, they can be unlearned. And though it is sometimes very difficult to imagine our nation totally free of racism and sexism, my intellect, my heart, and my experience tell me that it is actually possible. For that day when neither exists we must all struggle.

# On Being Black
# in America

*One ever feels his two-ness,—an American, a Negro; two souls, two thoughts, two unreconciled strivings; two warring ideals in one dark body, whose dogged strength alone keeps it from being torn asunder.*

*The history of the American Negro is the history of this strife,—this longing to attain self-conscious manhood, to merge his double self into a better and truer self. In this merging he wishes neither of the older selves to be lost. He would not Africanize America, for America has too much to teach the world and Africa. He would not bleach his Negro soul in a flood of white Americanism, for he knows that Negro blood has a message for the world. He simply wishes to make it possible for a man to be both a Negro and an American, without being cursed and spit upon by his fellows, without having the doors of Opportunity closed roughly in his face.*

—W.E.B. DU BOIS, "Of Our Spiritual Strivings,"
*The Souls of Black Folk* (1903)

PERHAPS MORE SO than at any other time, when Black History Month rolls around, African American women look back with pride and praise at the creativity of Phillis Wheatley, the daring of Harriet Tubman, the oratory of Sojourner Truth, the bravery of Ida B. Wells. We reflect on countless others—artists and activists, educators and entrepreneurs—who have made enormous contributions toward the empowerment of the African American community and the betterment of our nation. To the roll call of "sheroes" with name recognition we could easily add the names of thousands of lesser-known women.

As well we should, we celebrate these women as lights along the freedom trail, indicators of how far we have come. I sometimes fear, however, that we forget that we still have a long way to go. Today when an African American woman receives well-deserved recognition for excellence in a particular field of endeavor—the arts, the sciences, business, or education—she is often cheered not only for her specific accomplishment, but for being the *first* African American or the *first* African American woman to have done so. Even if we did not have a single statistic on the plight of African American women as a whole, the fact that we are still celebrating "firsts" is evidence that true equality has not yet been achieved. This means that here we stand on the edge of the twenty-first century and still we are not free. As has long been the case, our primary adversary is racism: the myth that we are innately inferior to White people, a myth that spawned and continues to spawn a horde of attitudes and actions that seek to ensure that our status in America remains that of second-class citizens.

There are of course those in our nation who disbelieve the ubiquitous presence of racism in our lives, who insist that the battle against racism has been won and that race is no longer an issue in the advancement of African Americans. There are African Americans as well as Whites who hold this position. In some cases people have confused the desegregation of public facilities and the progress of some individuals with the full incorporation of all African Americans into the life of our nation. Others toe this line out of a conditioned, willful blindness. After all, seeing is very disquieting. For one, injustice has a way of beckoning us to take corrective action which may require sacrifices that people generally do not wish to make. Moreover, "'fessing" up to racism in American rubs against the myth of America as the land of the free and the home of the brave. As they say, confession may be good for the soul but it is hard on the reputation. It is not surprising that African Americans who argue that racism is no longer a central force in our lives are received with open arms and rewarded with "good press," and the status of "expert." Their message is comforting to those in power who want to maintain the status quo, who would forge for us new chains by blocking progressive social legislation and cutting funding for programs that would rectify injustices.

Clichéd, but true, racism is alive and doing too well in America. Moreover, I do not view the faces of

CONVERSATIONS    55

racism as fundamentally different from times past.
As has always been the case, it runs the gamut from
blatant to more sophisticated expressions. Whenever
I hear commentary on the subtlety of today's racism,
I am quick to point out that there is nothing subtle
about savagely beating African American men in
Howard Beach, the brutal beating of Rodney King
by policemen, or sending a package-bomb to the
NAACP office in Jacksonville, Florida. Such atroci-
ties are also far from new: Remember Emmett Till?
Remember the little girls in Birmingham? Likewise,
the racial incidents on our college and university
campuses that were publicized in the last few years
are neither subtle nor markedly different from the
race-baiting and humiliations African Americans
have historically experienced at predominantly
White institutions of higher learning. Finally, if
there is one symbol of the most barbaric expression
of racism it is the Ku Klux Klan. The Klan marches
again. And the Klan has company: The Posse Comi-
tatus, Aryan Nations, White Aryan Resistance, and
other hate groups that preach White supremacy and
practice what they preach by terrorizing African
Americans, other people of color, and Jews. Sadly, as
in the past, religion is used to sanction and justify
racism. The "Identity" movement is a case in point.
As the Joint Center for Political and Economic Studies reported in the April 1990 issue of its newsletter,
*Focus:*

> According to a study conducted by the National Coun-
> cil of Churches Identity is a racist faith with a complete
> theology: blacks and other people of color are believed
> to be "pre-Adamic"—and therefore subhuman. Jews

are regarded as children of the devil. The doctrine goes on: racial integration is a sin, Armageddon will be a race war in the United States, for which whites must prepare by stockpiling weapons, food, etc. The faithful will be redeemed when the U.S. becomes a white Christian republic.

The writer describes Identity theology as the "spiritual glue that helps bind together large portions of the White supremacist movement" and quotes one sociologist as saying, "the danger to society from Identity exists precisely because it recruits from the mainstream of society rather than its margins."

We see sophisticated expressions of racism in attacks on affirmative action, civil rights laws, and scholarships for minority students which echo those attacks launched against gains African Americans made in the late nineteenth century during Reconstruction. In times past the press encouraged the fiction of the depravity of African Americans with florid tales and cartoons of our people as savages. There were sensationalistic "reports" of crimes that portrayed us as brutes. Today, some of mainstream media coverage of African American criminal suspects and offenders is profoundly reminiscent of the Scottsboro Boys.

African Americans are of course no longer legally classified as three-fifths of a person, but we continue to be discounted and negated in all things great and small, from consideration for top-level corporate and government positions to the labeling of pantyhose and adhesive bandages as "flesh-tone." (Whose flesh?) In the ordinary course of human interactions even the most well-intentioned of folk

make racist assumptions without even realizing it,
and such racism can appear when we least expect it.
Take the night my friend was sitting in the lobby of
the Princeton Club in New York City waiting for her
guest and was asked by the doorman, "Are you waiting for the cook?" Or take the evening a few years
ago when as a board member of the Atlanta Symphony Orchestra, I attended the symphony's annual
ball. There we were, my husband and I, having paid
$500 apiece and dressed in our best possible black-
tie outfits when a woman at our table asked me: "Are
you a member of the chorus?" These stories may not
evoke sympathy from all quarters; after all, my
friend could at least wrest out some semblance of an
apology, and after the ball my husband and I returned to the Spelman campus and the comfort of
our home. If we canvassed the African American
community at large, we could fill volumes with similar experiences and we would find, however, that in
many cases recovery from the insult was not so swift
or smooth as in the stories above. Consider the case
of a socially and economically disadvantaged Black
woman. When she suffers an assault on her dignity
from a social service worker, employer, coworker, or
merchant, what recourse does she have? What does
she go home to?

In revisiting the ways of racism in our lives I do
not minimize the progress that has been made toward a more racially enlightened society, nor do I
sneeze at the hard-earned victories of the Civil
Rights and Black Liberation movements. I simply
wish to warn against complacency and remind folk
that the battle is not over. Until it is, we are not free.

We have a collective sense that we are still not free.

The realization drifts around in the small places of our consciousness, bounces off the walls of our subconscious. For too many it remains, however, just "a sense," which we sometimes try to hope away, anything rather than look it straight in the eye and call its name.

As painful as it is to confront the fact that we are still not free, it is doubly painful to acknowledge what began it all. And yet, we can never understand America, nor can we ever understand Black America until we confront slavery. Confronting slavery means not only acknowledging the historical facts, but also slavery's collective damage to the psyche of African Americans. This, in turn, means recognizing that damage, if not repaired, is cumulative.

For this reason, not even the youngest generation can start the clock ticking with the Civil Rights movement. We must all start where it began: with the most unbelievably barbaric assault on humankind. W.E.B. Du Bois, one of the premier scholars, writers, and activists of the twentieth century, estimated that some 60 million women, men, and children were torn from the African shore. Sixty million is not just an extraordinary number; it is an extraordinary reality.

Whether or not you consciously acknowledge that you and yours began in slavery, whether or not you deliberately ground yourself in the history of slavery and its legacy (which you should, of course, do) is not the essential point. For the truth is that the historical and current condition of you and yours *is* rooted in it, *is* shaped by it, *is* bound to it, and *is* the reality against which all else must be gauged. The ancestors of every African American may not have been slaves, but the overwhelming majority were, which means that the overwhelming majority of us would not be African Americans were it not for slavery; and we all—descendants of enslaved and free Africans, alike—bear the mark of what happened to Africans granted open admissions into what mid-nineteenth-century Southerners euphemistically called a "Peculiar Institution."

Lest we forget whence we have come, let us imagine a West African woman in the last quarter of the eighteenth century brought to America to work like a draft animal and give birth to children destined to be exploited like draft animals, too. Remember that this woman is a citizen of a country that functions under a set of values, laws, and morals. She, like her countrymen, has more experience in civic decisions than the free White women then living in America. In terms of positions of authority, the historical record shows that several African women once governed in various regions of Africa with competency and imagination. Women such as Hatshepsut, who reigned as the first female pharaoh in Egypt from 1478 to 1457 B.C.; Makeda, Queen of Ethiopia and Saba (Sheba), fl.c. 960 to 930 B.C., and consort of Solomon; Nzingha, Queen of Ndongo (Angola) from 1623 to 1663, whom the Portuguese had to reckon with as a fierce warrior and shrewd negotiator. Most of the women stolen from Africa were not queens and warriors, but they had all been citizens in their societies; and even those who were slaves in their native lands had more rights than they would meet in America.

This West African woman is, by and large, well-educated. She has learned the roles, customs, rights, and limitations of women in her society and has been educated to an African cosmology and her role in it. She is bonded to her community and her fellow citizens by a common system of religion, morality, and social behavior that encompasses everything from whom she could marry to expected behavior of market women.

Without rehashing the horrors of the middle passage that involved human beings crammed into the hulls of ships, chained to each other, and forced to lie in their own excrement, let us imagine this woman caught up in a cataclysmic series of events when she arrives in America that literally strip her of her African self. Language, adornment, self-expression: Stripped! Rituals, relics, worship: Stripped! Modesty, protection from rape, and protection for her children: Stripped! Social status and legal redress: Stripped! Talents, knowledge, and skills . . . rendered useless.

This woman had not just been reduced from citizen to chattel, she has been subjected to a savaging of her person so horrible that her very personhood was violated and indeed negated. Under this barbaric system of slavery (the only point in American history when the unemployment rate for African Americans was 0 percent) this West African woman endured the excruciating pain of being slave labor no less than her male compatriot. And the lash she bore as well. Were concessions made if she were pregnant? Oh, yes. As a carrier of the next generation of "the master's" profit, she was made to put her extended belly into a deep hole so that the warm earth hugged and protected her baby while her back received the cold cruelty of the whip. As the brutal system dealt its blow to her by day, the night offered no respite in the most bitter sting of sexism: rape by "the master" and compulsory intercourse with an African man if she were branded a "good breeder." And because of the ideology of female subordination, sundown also meant another work shift: the burdens of household tasks in the slave cabin and the rearing of the slave children.

The term "underclass" may have gained wide currency during the 1980s, but an underclass—a segment of the populace basically devoid of economic and social power—is anything but new. This African woman brought to America, and her sisters, formed our first underclass and began life in America at the bottom of the slave class with no more rights than a brood mare.

Western Europeans and European Americans were long aware of the differences between themselves and Africans and may have had certain racist attitudes toward them, but they did not enslave this West African woman and her people because they simply did not like them or even because they hated them. In the accounts of Europeans who first went to Africa in the fifteenth century we find glowing reports of Africans as stately, well-mannered, highly civilized people. When Europeans further explored Africa and discovered there was much to be had there from gold to free labor, Africans were increasingly portrayed as barbarians and freaks of nature whose men were described as endowed with genitalia so large they required assistance in moving them and whose women fornicated with gorillas. The same people. What happened? An economic motive, or simply put: Greed. Slavery was more about free labor and profit than it was about racism, but slavery became a major reinforcer of racism and provided it with an institutional context in which to express itself. Racism continues to be profitable today. Naturally if you ask a merchant who overcharges African Americans, an employer who underpays them, or a landlord or landlady who neglects the property leased by African Americans, "Do you have racist attitudes because it is profitable?", they may look at you as if you were from the moon. A serious analysis, however, will reveal that unfounded but deeply ingrained notions about our inferiority to a large degree justify exploitation in the mind of the exploiter. The evidence seeps out in comments such as, "Black people don't expect any better"; or "Those people aren't going to know the difference."

In the 1960s we struggled not only to define racism, but to make the distinction between its institutionalized and individual expressions in order to better understand it and indeed to struggle against it. I think that is still a very important distinction to make. If racism were only a matter of beliefs, attitudes, and behavior of one, or two, or five hundred warped individuals, we could say, "It ain't such a big deal"; but it's more than that. Racism is dyed into the very cloth of the American way.

Countee Cullen's poem "Incident" tells of an eight-year-old African American boy who "Once riding in old Baltimore,/ Heart-filled, head-filled with glee" sees a little White boy staring at him. The African American boy smiles; the White child sticks out his tongue and calls him "Nigger." Concludes the little African American boy: "I saw the whole of Baltimore/ From May until December;/ Of all the things that happened there/ That's all that I remember."

As hurtful as it is to be called "Nigger," if this little boy and his little sister are only to experience racism on this level, in some sense it is manageable, because the African American community can soothe and comfort them. And while retaliation may not rank high among the virtues, the truth of the matter is that those children can vent their anger by sticking their tongues out and hurling back at that White child an insult or a more poignant memento.

Working with this same scenario, racism that is in-stitutionalized means that African Americans will not just be called "Nigger," but on every leg of their journey they will have less of a chance of reaching Baltimore, for there will be invisible road blocks that will impede, or worse, stop them. Even if we have the money for the ticket, we may find it difficult to purchase one; we may be ignored in the dining car; or our car may be mysteriously disconnected from the other cars and derailed at some point before we get to Baltimore. Baltimore may be the ability to purchase a home in a neighborhood one can afford, securing a business loan or credit from wholesalers, getting a promotion, making law partner, holding public office, or becoming executive editor at a mainstream publishing company. And for those who do make it to Baltimore, oftentimes it is impossible to calculate the real price of the ticket they may have had to pay.

With institutional racism one is fighting against formations that are far larger and less tangible than a single individual. Frustration mounts all the more because you can't beat up an institution, any more than you can beat up a train. One of the difficulties that arises when you cannot beat up an institution is that you begin to internalize the oppressor's estimation of you and begin striving to be acceptable and therefore accepted. This is what fuels the belief of many African Americans that if they earn an Ivy League degree, purchase a summer home in a predominantly White resort community, or make a lot of money they will be spared racist attitudes and behavior. In naïveté these people are saying, "You see, I am not what you think. I am not like the others." But as many have found, they are still so often perceived through racist-colored glasses.

Efforts to identify with the oppressor and prove oneself worthy are accompanied by self-denial and self-deprecation because it is difficult if not impossible to embrace one image of oneself without letting a conflicting one go. This stripping of oneself takes many and diverse forms, from out-and-out "passing" to disassociating oneself from one's people and aspects of one's cultural heritage. And, of course, there are efforts to physically transform one's very appearance.

We do not know for how many, but surely for some African American women shame and self-denial are at play when they straighten their hair; line their lips to make them appear thinner; use, less so today than in times past, bleaching creams; more recently, undergo cosmetic surgery to de-Africanize their features; and turn to contact lenses in pursuit of (like Toni Morrison's Pecola Breedlove) the bluest eye.

To say that every African American woman who, for example, straightens her hair is denying herself is simply not true. But if such is accompanied by other symbols of self-denial, one has to stop and question it. I doubt that many African American women have at some point in their life stood before a mirror and said, "I hate my hair because it is the antithesis of White women's hair. Let me go out and try to get White women's hair." On some level it is a matter of habit, on another, of fashion. At the same time, however, we cannot let slide by the argument that straightened hair, and blue, green, or hazel contact lenses are merely fashion statements. One must ask, "Why is it fashionable?" Answer: Because this society says that what is fashionable is to look as White as you can look. And what is fashionable is considered beautiful.

Lest anyone is tempted to pick up this discussion and run with it toward a theory that singles out African American women as the sole perpetrators of self-denial, I must emphasize that such actions are part of a common syndrome of oppressed people. Many a Jewish woman has had her nose broken and "bobbed" in an effort to be more "fashionable"; every year, and increasingly so, large numbers of Asian American women endure a very painful operation to reduce the slant in their eyes. And as James Baldwin reminded us in *The Price of the Ticket*,[1] for years Europeans have been literally or figuratively coming through Ellis Island, "where *Giorgio* becomes *Joe, Pappavasiliu* becomes *Palmer, Evangelos* becomes *Evans, Goldsmith* becomes *Smith* or *Gold,* and *Avakian* becomes *King.* So, with a painless change of name, and in the twinkling of an eye, one becomes a white

[1] New York: St. Martin's/Mark, 1985.

American. . . . The price the white American paid for his ticket was to become white. . . ." For the overwhelming majority of us to become literally White would be a most impossible dream, which makes our figurative attempts all the more pathetic and painful, namely because they do not work.

At the same time that oppression can lead people to disavow themselves, it can also bring about a rather perverse sense of solidarity. As was the case years ago, whenever we hear of a horrible crime that has been committed, we immediately wonder, "Is it one of us?" In times past the fear was that other African Americans would be made to pay for the deeds of one. In the days of unabashed White terror, this was a matter of no small consequence. Today, we ask "Is it one of us?" because even if we don't fear physical retribution, we know the many may be judged on the basis of the actions of a few. In the logic of stereotypes the misdeeds of one African American are used as "evidence" for the incompetency or immorality of all African Americans. This strange sense of solidarity often makes us feel compelled to defend people who do not deserve it. At other times we feel responsible for making the race look good. We see this in a matter as trivial as tipping. Many African Americans have told me that they often overtip taxi drivers and waiters to "make it good" for the next African American who comes behind them and to combat the stereotype that African Americans are poor tippers.

This sense of immediate identification comes into play in our triumphs as well. I remember my stomach hurting when Jackie Robinson would come up to bat. Not only because if he struck out it was as if all Black folk had done just that, but also because his home runs belonged to all of us. I no less remember hearing my parents say that when Marian Anderson sang on the steps of the Lincoln Memorial on Easter Sunday 1939 after the Daughters of the American Revolution refused her permission to sing at Constitution Hall, it was as if all Black people had spoken out in a song. And I know many an African American who watched the 1988 Olympics felt they had won when Florence Griffith-Joyner captured one silver and three gold medals in track and field events. For African American women it was an incredible victory because it is so rare for one of us to be projected internationally. Another factor in our celebration of "Flo Jo" is that she represents an exceptional merger of femininity and athletic ability. How can you be that beautiful and run that fast? Our sister defied the notion that a beautiful woman is necessarily shallow and an intelligent or highly skilled woman is inevitably physically unattractive.

But there is still something pathetic about all of this. It is as if there are so few opportunities for success that the many have to live vicariously off the successes of the few, and assumptions about the abilities of most of us are based on what one among us has or has not achieved.

Some declare that bondage is a state of mind. Many of our forebears might take unction at this and find it rather flippant; nevertheless there is some truth to these words because when we consider all the head trips we go through, we see that racism is in large measure a form of psychological warfare.

To be sure, racism is no respecter of gender. African American men and women have received their unfair share of its blows. But there are particular stings the African American woman has known. If human beings are anything we are multidimensional, but the African American woman's image has been distorted by a complex of stereotypes which, as stereotypes are designed to do, cast complex and diverse human beings into simpleminded singularities. Racist stereotypes are far more damaging than simply being "called outta your name." They are subtle means of manipulation and control, allowing the victimizers to blame the victims and justify their inhumanity toward them.

Of all the stereotypes about African American women, the most pervasive and damaging are those which cast us as either the good and faithful servant, the whore, or the matriarch. It is interesting to note that to varying degrees these stereotypes are bound up with the issue of sex and sexuality.

The Mammy, usually fat and almost always grinning, shoulders everyone's burdens and becomes everyone's workhorse. Although she may lactate, she is often viewed as a neuter being; and if she is seen as neither man nor woman, chances are she'll be treated like a beast. White Southerners' portrayals of domestic servants as willing workers justified and whitewashed their abusive treatment of them. Mammy did not fade away with slavery. As historian Deborah Gray White explained in *Ar'n't I a Woman?: Female Slaves in the Plantation South:*

> As the Old South's last generation penned memoir after memoir, the nation showed an increasing willingness to accept the South's point of view about plantation slavery before the Civil War. In the pictures

painted by Americans, Mammy towered behind every orange blossom, mint julep, erring white child, and gracious Southern lady. She was immortalized in D. W. Griffith's popular antiblack film, *Birth of a Nation,* and eight years after its 1915 debut, the Daughters of the American Confederacy petitioned Congress to erect a granite monument in Mammy's likeness in Washington so that all Americans could pay tribute to her. The petition did not go far in Congress but in the 1930s, 1940s, and 1950s Hollywood film producers and New York advertising agencies built their own monuments to Mammy. With their films, their pancake boxes, and their syrup bottles, they imprinted the image of Mammy on the American psyche more indelibly perhaps than ever before. We probably can not measure the effect of the mass packaging of Mammy with precision, but the fact is that Mammy became a national symbol of perfect domesticity at the very time that millions of black women were leaving the cotton fields of the South in search of employment in Northern urban areas. Surely there is some connection between the idea of Mammy, the service and domestic jobs readily offered to black women, and their near-exclusion from other kinds of work.[2]

Alongside Mammy hangs the portrait of the oversexed Jezebel. This image of the promiscuous temptress has made African American women open game for more disrespect and sexual harassment, from leers to more forceful advances, than White women would ever know. Deborah Gray White also offers an excellent analysis of just how damaging this stereotype has been:

[2] New York: W. W. Norton, 1985.

From emancipation through more than two-thirds of the twentieth century, no Southern white male was convicted of raping or attempting to rape a black woman. Yet the crime was so widespread that the staff of the National Commission on the Causes and Prevention of Violence admitted in 1969 that the few reported instances of the crime reflected not the crime's low incidence but the fact that "white males have long had nearly institutionalized access to Negro women with relatively little fear of being reported." Black women had almost as little recourse to justice when the perpetrator was black. When a black man raped a black woman, police consistently reported the crime as "unfounded," and in relatively few cases that reached the courts, the testimony of black female victims was seldom believed by white juries.

It is worth noting that there is also a racial-sexual stereotype of African American men as studs; and yet this stereotype is an ambiguous one. The notion of Black men as studs makes some White people paranoid that African American men will rape White women. Simultaneously there is a certain amount of admiration in White America for the "big Black stud" which makes this stereotype, albeit deplorable, not totally negative. But you don't dress up the whore. You just use and abuse her.

Sapphire completes the triptych. This castrating, domineering woman who runs her husband out and then runs their home and children achieved "credibility" of course in *The Negro Family: The Case for National Action*, commonly referred to as "The Moynihan Report," which maintained that it had found the enemy of the Black family and it is the Black matriarchy. If it were not so damning, the concept of

the Black matriarchy would be laughable because it
is a truly prizewinning oxymoron in a society which
by design and structure denies power to people of
color and withholds as much as possible from
women. Nevertheless the legend lives.

This image of African American women as Sap-
phires not only compromises our humanity in wider
society, it also jeopardizes our relationships with African American men because (like the "twofer" or
two-for-one myth) it makes us scapegoats for their
oppression.

These pervasive stereotypes about African American women also have unfortunate consequences in
terms of our own behavior. Oftentimes they put us
in a defensive position and make us feel guilty about
our accomplishments and for exhibiting healthy
attributes. To be nurturing and caring is good, as it
is to be self-sufficient, independent, and liberated
from unproductive, old-fashioned mores about sex.
But in the case of the African American woman, in
displaying these positive qualities she is aware that
she is likely to be viewed (and thus treated!) as a
Mammy, a Jezebel, a Sapphire.

Another pain African American women have had
to bear is bound up in our relationship with White
women, who historically by and large have had no
quarrel with racism. A very important piece of the
history of African American women is in "Miss
Anne's kitchen," early on as slaves, later as maids, or
rather, as some preferred to put it, as Miss Anne's
"girls." Life in Miss Anne's house meant long hard
hours of cooking, cleaning, washing, ironing, and
rocking her babies. In recompense Black women
were given little pay and a great deal of disrespect.

Being given hand-me-down clothes and scraps from "her lady's" table hardly made matters all right. Although African American men experienced racism at the hands of White women, it was a double slap in the face for African American women because they knew that White women were likewise victims of a form of oppression. They looked expectantly to White women to cease and desist from oppressing them. Although African American women are no longer in Miss Anne's kitchen in the numbers we once were, the experiences of those who were and still are remain fresh in our collective memory. As White women persist in racist behavior toward African American women, African American women, whether on their knees scrubbing the floor, in front of a typewriter, or at a conference table, will continue to look up and out at White women and say, "But why you? You of all people should know what it feels like to be oppressed."

Racism has had a particular sting for African American women who are mothers, an agony captured in Margaret Burroughs' poem "What Shall I Tell My Children Who Are Black?" As long as we women are the primary caretakers of children more often than not, it is to us that little girls and boys come crying when they are hurt. One of the most profoundly painful emotions in the world is when an African American mother is confronted with her child's hurt from racism. This experience is inevitable. Even if the child attends an elite preparatory school or lives in a "liberal" neighborhood, that child is going to be hurt by racism. When a child asks, "Mama, what's a Nigger?" or says, "Mama, Joanie said her parents told her not to play with me," the pain and frustration a mother experiences is almost indescribable. What should she tell her child who is Black? An enormous tribute is owed African American parents, particularly mothers, who for years have had the responsibility of providing balm for the wounds racism inflicted upon their children and the task of counseling them on how to weave their way through and around its horrors.

I must admit, I am tired of talking about racism, and even more exhausted with experiencing it. These emotions put me in close touch with millions of African Americans I have never seen, of whose names, addresses, occupations, and particular life circumstances I know nothing. At the same time I am obviously not tired of fighting against racism. I know that this, too, puts me in touch with millions of African Americans who carry with them the legacy of African American resistance: from sabotaging the sugarcane mill and orchestrating work slowdowns in the cotton fields to engineering the underground railroad and planning slave revolts. Indeed, as someone once said, where there is oppression there is resistance.

This precept was at the heart of a final exam essay question I often posed when I taught a course on "The Anthropology of Afro-American Culture." The question was this: "Imagine that tomorrow you wake up and there is no more racism. Will Afro-American culture still exist?" The question was based on the principle that one way that people resist oppression is to consciously and unconsciously reaffirm themselves. That is to say that because we have been " 'buked and scorned" there is a very serious and complex affirmation of ourselves through much of our literature, music, painting, even our body language as in the definitive way in which an African American woman can suck through her teeth, put her hands on her hips, and dismiss a notion (or a person) quicker than you can bat an eye.

The question really unsettled students. First, because it underscored just how constrained our lives are by racism, and second because the question ultimately asks: What is there that is positive about African American life that is not created in reaction to racism? How do we know what our creativity would be were it not there? (There's absolutely no reason to assume that it would not flower.)

I ask you, my sisters, to imagine that tomorrow you awaken and not only is racism no more, but its history has been erased from the national consciousness. How would your life change? What would you do differently? Would you ever think twice about criticizing another African American in front of White people? Would you still think you have to be twice as good? Do you think you would be treated differently in your workplace, in your school? What would you do with the energy once spent trying to figure out whether someone is a racist or simply a grouch? Would there be a noticeable decrease of tension in your mind, body, and soul?

If these questions find any resonance within you and set off a spark of idealism, they might then move you to link spirits, so to speak, with Langston Hughes in "I Dream a World," a dream he surely had for all women as well as men.

> I dream a world where man
> No other will scorn,

Where love will bless the earth
And peace its paths adorn.
I dream a world where all
Will know sweet freedom's way,
Where greed no longer saps the soul
Nor avarice blights our day.
A world I dream where black or white,
Whatever race you be,
Will share the bounties of the earth
And every man is free,
Where wretchedness will hang its head,
And joy, like a pearl,
Attend the needs of all mankind.
Of such I dream—
Our world![3]

If in these last few moments you have been able to dream a world, a better world, where racism no longer exists, then you must also be prepared to respond to the question, "What are you willing to do to make this vision a reality?" While it is true that without a vision the people perish, it is doubly true that without action the people and their vision perish as well.

To put forth a ten-point directive to eradicate racism is not only bold, it is inane, for each must examine herself and reexamine the road she has traveled to determine what she can and will do.

On a very immediate level, we African American women, along with our brothers, can more vocally and pointedly fight racism by calling it wherever we see it. If you are present when someone makes a

___

[3] An aria from the opera *Troubled Island* with a score by William Grant Still, n.d.

remark or an assumption that stems from a racist perspective on the world and your role in it, for your own well-being and "the good of the race"—if not for his or her enlightenment—it is incumbent upon you to correct their analysis. Ideally this should be undertaken with a spirit of grace, and common sense should of course be your guide in terms of the when, where, how, and if of the matter. At the same time, I would be less than honest if I did not acknowledge that there will be occasions when you may be compelled to "read" somebody without regard to considerations of propriety. Similarly, if you come across a product that in its labeling, instructions, or packaging is blindly Eurocentric, my sister, you really should write the manufacturer or company and inform it that using certain terms makes an assumption and is fundamentally racist. Calling it wherever you see it, albeit laborious, is salutary because it is an act of self-affirmation if nothing else. Although you may not affect another's attitude, you may at least change their behavior. This change of behavior, if consistent, may, down the road, have an effect on the individual's heart and mind.

The theory of cognitive dissonance maintains that human beings do not operate well when there is dissonance between their behavior and their attitudes. Something has to change. Thus when written and unwritten laws prevent individuals from engaging in racist behavior there is at least the possibility that they will change their racist attitudes in order to get out of a state of discord. Hypothetically speaking, if it were illegal to call an African American "Nigger," a racist, being forced to suppress the impulse to use the epithet may eventually purge him- or herself of racist attitudes. Bearing this theory in mind, it therefore behooves you not only to "call it wherever you see it," my sister, but to fight for anti-discrimination legislation. Of course, there will be some who will continue to live in dissonance. That is, they will not call you Nigger but they will still think it. Others may keep their behavior in line with their attitudes, that is they will call you Nigger and face the penalty. For the good of African Americans and the nation as a whole, we must continue to pressure our government for strong anti-discrimination laws, thereby setting up at least the possibility that a greater proportion of people will change their attitudes. And what shall we do about those who continue to live in dissonance or those who decide to break the law? We should pray for the former because to live in dissonance is painful. We should do our utmost to avoid the latter, for these are truly dangerous human beings.

As important as it is for African Americans to move against racism in the public arena, it no less important to do some "homework." As the principal caretakers of African American children, African American women can be the primary and perhaps ultimately the most effective socializers of resistance. This is not to absolve African American men from all responsibility of socializing our children—whether it is to teach them about racism, or how to tie their shoes. It is simply to be realistic about who is the first and most influential instructor for most of our young—African American women.

While you may not want to socialize your child to be combative and confrontational, if you do not instill in that child the principle that being called Nigger—literally and subliminally—is not acceptable, then you are not rearing that child well. Raising our children well first requires us to teach them that they are not inferior and then to encourage them to have the confidence to speak out against racism. Even if it is in the third or fourth grade, a child who senses that a teacher is saying something that is fundamentally racist needs to have the necessary tools to deal with it in a manner befitting the moment. If not, then we are setting that child up for self-denial, self-deprecation, and participation in his or her own oppression.

Lessons on the realities of racism need not be grueling propaganda sessions. The issue can be addressed, for example, in analyses of the way African Americans are portrayed in news and entertainment media. "Deprogramming" can be conducted by gently but firmly correcting your child when he or she makes a comment or is in earshot of one that is self-deprecatory: "nappy-headed" or "she's pretty for a dark-skinned girl" or "Black people just ain't ready," should not be a part of your child's vocabulary or consciousness. Nipping these things in the bud may seem tedious and time-consuming, but if we do not do so the bud will surely blossom. As we instruct our children on the realities of racism and its effect on our lives we would do well to instruct them against participating or condoning racial and ethnic bigotry against others. This is to say that African Americans can ill afford to make anti-Semitic jokes, propagate prejudiced views of Puerto Ricans, harbor anti-Asian sentiments, or believe in Lone Ranger images of Native Americans.

The precept of doing unto others as you would have them do unto you may have a greater chance of hitting home with White women than with White men. Although the gulf between most Black and White women is indeed wide, to the extent that gender-bonding can occur because of shared experiences with sexism, African American women have the opportunity and the responsibility to raise the consciousness of White women on racism. If African American women can do this in private conversation or public discussion, they will in effect have raised the consciousness of a generation. For after all, White women are the primary caretakers and socializers of White children.

For African American women to challenge racism on any front will of course first require that we truly acknowledge that it exists, and that it is not an abstract phantom but a very powerful force in our lives. Some will advise against this with comments such as, "We've come a long way, get on with your life!" Of course you should get on with your life, but you should never deny reality.

Denying and forgetting are, on some level, survival mechanisms. As we know from the stories of victims of physical and sexual abuse, coping and surviving often means blocking out reality. We also know that continuous blocking will do long-term emotional damage, whereas remembering and confronting reality is one of the most profoundly human and ultimately healing experiences. I think back to my trip to Israel in 1962 and my visit to a memorial museum on the Holocaust. At that site, as I read the words "Lest we forget," I thought, "It really is all right that I do not want people to forget about slavery and racism. It is human to insist on remembering." And it seems to me that the experience of slavery and racism have been so chilling to the bone that even when they cease we will still have to remember to sing those songs, if only to express how wonderful life is that racism no longer lives.

# Between a Rock
# and a Hard Place

## On Being Black
## and a Woman

*The colored woman of to-day occupies, one may say, a unique position in this country. In a period of itself transitional and unsettled, her status seems one of the least ascertainable and definitive of all the forces which make for our civilization. She is confronted by both a woman question and a race problem, and is as yet an unknown or an unacknowledged factor in both.*

—Anna Julia Cooper, "The Status of Woman in America," *A Voice from the South* (1892)

*As a Black woman/feminist, I must look about me, with trembling, and with shocked anger, at the endless waste, the endless suffocation of my sisters: the bitter sufferings of hundreds of thousands of women who are the sole parents, the mothers of hundreds of thousands of children, the desolation and the futility of women trapped by demeaning, lowest-paying occupations, the unemployed, the bullied, the beaten, the battered, the ridiculed, the slandered, the trivialized, the raped, and the sterilized, the lost millions and multimillions of beautiful, creative, and momentous lives turned to ashes on the pyre of gender identity. I must look about me and, as a Black feminist, I must ask myself:* Where is the love? *How is my own lifework serving to end these tyrannies, these corrosions of sacred possibility?*

—June Jordan, "Where Is the Love?" *Civil Wars* (1981)

LIKE RACISM, sexism is an irrational leap of faith from recognizing differences to believing that difference makes a qualitative difference. To complete the parallel, the ideology of female inferiority has bred attitudes, beliefs, and behavior that promote the subordination and oppression of women.

The idea that female subordination has always existed and is inevitable is frightful, and, frankly, depressing because it implies that being oppressed and being an oppressor are natural and acceptable states of humanity. This line of reasoning says, in effect, that a little girl is born to be ruled and a little boy emerges from the womb ready, willing, and able to dominate his sister and her female friends. This position flies in the face of the fact that in certain precolonial Native American and West African societies, for example, women and men lived under greater degrees of gender equality than we know today in America. And obviously, it contradicts the reality that now in America there is less sex discrimination than in the past.

Clearly sexism, like racism, is neither genetic nor irreversible. Nor do I believe it is the divinely ordained and righteous order of the universe. The truth of the matter is, however, that sexism has a certain social acceptability precisely because it has theological moorings. But one must bear in mind that the gatekeepers of religion have traditionally been men and that even those with the best intentions have served us theologies that, as womanist theologian Jacqueline Grant put it, "have emerged out of the experiences of only one-half of the human race. . . ."[1] These theologies have, I believe, through distortions and faulty interpretations sanctioned sexism. I do not wish to offend anyone's religious sensibilities or upset anyone's theological applecart, but I do believe that as Grant also points out, we need to "bring about a more realistic and wholistic picture of the universe by developing a more wholistic theology."[2] Such a theology would prove liberating and healthy for everyone, but especially for "Eve's descendants," because the existence of sexism has been and continues to be a nightmare reality for millions of women.

The supposition that women are "less than" men was realized most egregiously in written and unwritten laws that established a daughter as her father's property and a wife as her husband's. Sexism has played itself out in the lives of women by spurring men to deny women access to knowledge, entrance into certain professions and positions of authority solely on the basis of gender. Demeaning and fallacious analyses of women as helpless, vacuous "little creatures" were manufactured to justify and bolster male domination. Of course, time and time again women have proven the "theories" wrong. But until very recently there has been a virtual "news blackout" on such women. Even today, competitive, competent, intrepid women are oftentimes seen, at best,

---

[1] *White Women's Christ and Black Women's Jesus: Feminist Christology and Womanist Response* (Atlanta: Scholars Press, 1989).

[2] Ibid.

as exceptions to the rule and, at worst, as perversions of nature.

Not every woman's "adventure" with sexism has been the same. There have always been enlightened men and oppression-intolerant women. Moreover, economics has played a role in the tone and timbre of the oppression a woman experienced: the agony and frustration of a lady of leisure in Poshville, USA, does not compare to that of a poor woman in Pitstown tethered to hearth and home as a beast of burden.

When sexism is then superimposed not only on poverty but on racism, we find the worst nightmare of all. For according to the "logic" of oppression, if African Americans are less than Whites and women are less than men, then African American women are least of all—least of all even among their sisters of color. Perhaps it will be more fully appreciated here as opposed to in my earlier discussion of racism, that with White American racism there is a definitive hierarchy that positions other people of color —Asians, Hispanics, Native Americans—above people of African descent. To a large extent the wild card in all of this is phenotype: what you look like, plain and simple. Of course the hierarchical plot thickens among Black folks such that some people perceive light-skinned African Americans with what we might call Euro-hair as still "less than" Whites and other people of color, but certainly better than their darker brethren and sistren with "woolly locks."

African American women, confronted with racism on the one hand and sexism on the other, find themselves, indeed, between a rock and a hard place. Although we have been more preoccupied with the weight of racism, we are keenly aware of the oppression we experience as women. This awareness is not limited to the "intellectuals" among us; and though it may not be articulated in the tribal language of academia, it is expressed. Some years ago this point was vividly brought home to me when I heard a formally uneducated woman declare: "Lissen, honey, it don't make no difference if it's the man out there messin' with you or it's the man in your house." And she added: "Let me tell you something, ain't nobody catch it like us Black women."

Needless to say, one of the most painful moments in our lives is when, whether in the kitchen, at the typewriter, or at the conference table we turn to an African American man and ask, "But why you? You of all people should know what it feels like to be oppressed." Of course, African American men know full well intellectually and experientially what it feels like to be oppressed by both White men and White women. It is therefore understandable—*but definitely unconscionable*—that some African American men vent their anger and pain by asserting their "manhood" on African American women. It is the classic chain reaction of frustration: The owner verbally pounces on the manager who screams at the assistant manager who goes home and yells at his wife who in turn chastises a child who then kicks the dog.

The phrase "battle of the sexes" is in a sense deplorable because it is very close to notions of physical abuse—the most extreme manifestation of the phrase and a distinct reality for all too many women. There is, however, an inevitable tension that flares up when a man wants to dominate a woman and that woman does not want to be dominated; and trouble will surely come when a man strives to maintain power, and a woman seeks to gain her fair share. Yet, a peaceful, more equitable and more civilized coexistence can be reached with the furtherance of feminism. Feminism is quite simply the antidote to sexism. But like many ideologies and movements—from Socialism to Pan-Africanism to Utopianism—feminism has been grossly and woefully misunderstood.

The feminist movement is based on the belief that men and women are equal as human beings. In other words, Nona is not inevitably the typist (or now the "word processor") and Nick is not inevitably the boss. Feminism insists that women should receive equal pay for equal work, have decision-making power when it comes to their own bodies, and enjoy the opportunity to participate fully in the political life of their communities and their nation. Feminism presupposes that women are capable of driving cars well, solving complex mathematical problems, and playing a saxophone. Feminism challenges the assumption that Lincoln University, the University of Chicago, Bennett College, the University of Wisconsin, Spelman College, or any company or organization will run amuck because they have women at the helm.

Feminism contends that although men do not give birth to children, they are quite capable of loving and rearing them because genetically there is nothing that keeps them from being nurturing, caring human beings. Feminism hopes that men like women will help sons and daughters with their homework, visit sick relatives in the hospital, and remember Grandma's birthday when it comes around. Feminism shudders at the notion that "real men" don't cry, don't sew on buttons, and don't do a thousand and one other things in the bogus category of "unmanly."

To champion the cause of an elevated and egalitarian status for both genders is not to deny differences. Social scientists are now suggesting that there are different ways that women and men see, know, think, and feel. It is being argued, for example, that as managers, women are far more consultative and far less concerned with hierarchy within an office than are men. When these theories call on a biological explanation for such differences, I part company with them. However, the idea seems a sound one if its basis is that men and women see, know, think, and feel differently because they are socialized so very differently.

One of the knee-jerk reactions to feminist thought has been the accusation that it not only denies differences between the genders, but also seeks to obliterate them. Some would blame feminism for the androgynous trend in clothing and hairstyles. But why shouldn't a woman have a pinstripe suit in her wardrobe alongside an evening gown and a man have fuchsia and canary-yellow shirts side by side his white button-downs? I think we should be grateful that more and more people are violating traditional dress codes. This is especially true for women because so much of what is deemed "feminine" clothing is designed to perpetuate the image of women as sex objects. Androgynous couture and coiffure have little, however, to do with feminism. Feminism does not preach that we all ought to dress alike, look alike, or talk alike. It simply purports that every human being should have the liberty to express his or her preferences and potential without constraint or reproach, as long as in doing so the rights of others are not violated. Feminism does not call for androgyny; it calls for equality.

Another false charge hurled at feminism is that it advocates a total role reversal between the genders. For example, a critic of feminism passing by a construction site might contend that a feminist wants all the construction workers to be women and all their menfolk to be house-husbands. A true feminist response is: If there are women capable of doing such work who want to do such work, then . . . let them do it! Likewise, if there are men who want to be homemakers, hats off to them, too. The idea that there is any more to it than this is nonsense. Equally ridiculous is the charge that feminists want to do away with acts of courtesy.

There is nothing fundamentally wrong or offensive about, for example, opening a door for someone. I must say that on more than one occasion, while leaving a meeting, a man has moved to open a door for me but stopped short and said (often facetiously), "Oh, I'm not sure you're going to like that." A balanced feminist response to this is that whoever is nearest the door should open it, or whoever is encumbered with packages should not be the one to do so. The important point on this and other expressions of civility is that men and women alike are deserving of them. I think that a feminist's refusal to have a door opened for her is a defensive act triggered by the knowledge that the perception of women as "the weaker sex" often undergirds this gesture. And so, refusing to have a door opened for one is a way of saying, "I am not helpless." On a more symbolic level these women are also saying, "Leave this door. Why don't you open the real doors?"—the real doors being those that lead to positions of significance within a company or organization and allow a woman to advance at the same rate of speed as a man with equal qualifications. The symbolism, however, is often missed.

I am not a betting woman, but I would venture to say that one would have to search high and low to find large numbers of African American women who disagree with the fundamental goals of feminism. I believe that because of our "adventure" with racism we have a deep and abiding attachment to equality that extends to all dimensions of being. Hence, I think many of us automatically embrace feminism even though we may reject the word. When a woman is angry and says "I am doing exactly the same job as this guy in my office and doing it just as well, why is he getting more money than I am?" that is a feminist question. (A nonfeminist accepts that she is paid less *because* she is a woman.) When a woman asks her mate, "What makes you think I am any less tired than you? I worked a full day just like you did. I don't see why you get to sit down, drink beer, and watch a baseball game while I cook dinner, get the children washed, and straighten up the house," that is a feminist talking.

Although many African American women subscribe to the basic principles of feminism, the truth of the matter is that *feminist* is not a word that sits comfortably with the vast majority of us, nor a movement to which in large numbers we consciously and

actively pledge our allegiance. The reasons are multiple: among them, the tactics of anti-feminists to dis-
credit the movement, the behavior of some White
feminists, and, to a certain extent, the shortsighted-
ness of African American women.

I would venture to say that next to *communist* there
are few words that the media and conservatives have
been so successful at turning people against as the
word *feminist*. When the second wave of the
Women's movement took hold in the late 1960s and
1970s, the press that presented feminists as man-haters and bra-burners looking for hard-hats was devastating. The slant on the coverage of the Women's
movement was so negative that, understandably,
many a woman must have thought, I don't want to
be one of *them!* If that were not enough, much of the
media projected the movement as the crusade not
only of man-haters and bra-burners but of lesbians
as well.

African American women have not escaped the
profound homophobia that grips American society.
Perhaps the most unspoken but deep-seated fear of
many African American women is that any association with feminism will be construed as evidence of
lesbianism. Of course, and as well there should be,
there were and are lesbians in the Women's movement; and perhaps because of the duality of their
oppression as women and as homosexuals, they
have been among the most vocal advocates of gender equality. But the proportion of lesbians and gay
men in the African American community is no more
and no less than in American society as a whole and
to equate feminism with lesbianism is as false as defining civil rights as racial separatism.

In addition to the stigma the media attached to the feminist movement, African American women's disaffection stems from issues revolving around race and racism. Historically, for most White women "Women's Liberation" has meant "White Women's Liberation": So impenetrable was their racism, they were unable to see African American women as women, too. When they did include us—sometimes out of enlightenment, but often, for political expediency—our contributions, interests, and sensibilities were shoved to the periphery if kept in view at all. For example, in commemorating nineteenth-century and early twentieth-century pioneers in the Women's movement, latter-day feminists excluded images of African Americans such as Ida B. Wells, Mary Church Terrell, Anna Julia Cooper, and Mary McLeod Bethune. Just as African American women were given subordinate status in the Civil Rights and Black Liberation movements and our concerns and needs were by and large ignored, so it was within the Women's movement. The title and jacket line of an anthology on Black Women's Studies says it best: *All the Women Are White, All the Blacks Are Men, But Some of Us Are Brave.*[3] The cryptic quality of this title emphasizes the invisibility African American women have suffered in their quest for equality.

Many African American women approached feminism with suspicion because one of the standard phrases of the women's movement proclaimed that we women are "all sisters!" That pronouncement was often followed by the assertion that raising differences among us is divisive. But as poet Audre

[3] Edited by Gloria T. Hull, Patricia Bell Scott, and Barbara Smith (Old Westbury, N.Y.: The Feminist Press, 1982).

Lorde has said: ". . . it is not difference which im-mobilizes us, but silence. And there are so many si-lences to be broken."[4] As much as the conditions and experiences of White women, African American women, and other women of color may be similar, there are very important differences in our circum-stances and experiences, differences that defy singu-lar analyses of women's oppression and blanket dic-tums about how to achieve gender equality.

Much of the feminist movement of the 1970s re-volved around the call for women to work. This was an obvious opportunity for White feminists to ac-knowledge the differences among women, but they failed to do so. The battle cry, "Out of the house and into the marketplace," struck African American women as quite absurd because we have always worked—and often, in the homes of the grandmoth-ers, mothers, sisters and aunts of these very women who seemed to have just discovered the workplace we have always known. For many African American women, a chance not to work outside the home was seen as a luxury. In addition, for many African American women the opportunity to stay at home meant a respite from the racial oppression they ex-perienced in the marketplace, not to mention the sexual harassment they endured if they were domes-tic workers.

There is a saying, "All lies are based on a bit of truth." Clearly the Women's movement of the early 1970s was not exclusively composed of bra-burners and man-haters. However there were some feminists

[4] "The Transformation of Silence into Language and Action," in *Sister Outsider: Essays and Speeches* (Freedom, Calif.: The Crossing Press, 1984).

who burned their bras and, yes, trashed men. It is the latter action that most African American women have found unacceptable. Although we have certainly experienced domineering attitudes and behaviors of African American men, we have consistently watched White society victimize our fathers, brothers, mates, and sons. Racism, then, creates an inevitable bond between African American men and women that many White feminists overlook, either willfully or out of sheer ignorance.

Racism within the feminist movement and the failure of many White feminists to recognize and understand the differences between our respective historical and current realities resulted in a customized brand of feminism that African American women *ought* to have rejected. At the same time, when confronted with progressive and enlightened White feminists, many African American women hesitated to link arms with these women because we were in a sense blinded by their Whiteness: so vivid is the memory of their participation in our oppression, in deed (as savage taskmasters themselves) and in their silent consent (as expressed in their failure to oppose slavery and segregation) that African American women were hard-pressed to trust even earnest and sincere White feminists. This distrust is not solely based on the evidence of things once seen. For today we still find White women who issue a clarion call for gender equality but continue to pay their housekeepers (among them African Americans) insulting wages, and who march for abortion rights but never for civil rights.

Finally, one of the major reasons African American women failed to become involved in the feminist movement in greater numbers is because we have been so profoundly engaged by the onslaughts of racism and the necessity to fight it that every other struggle became secondary. In part, this also explains why many of us are blind to notions of class. We have spent so much of our collective life looking at the world in racial terms that we fail to see other bases of oppression.

Unfortunately, in absenting ourselves from the mainstream feminist movement many African American women threw out the baby with the bathwater: In our myopia a great many have—much to our detriment—taken the position that feminist issues are not our issues. The failure to organize in greater numbers against rape with or apart from other women is our loss because African American women are raped more often than White women. How can the issue of equal pay be solely a White woman's issue when African American women are on the bottom of the pay scale? And too many of us have failed to see that pornography is an industry that traffics in the dehumanization of *all* women. Clearly, pornography becomes our issue, too. Regardless of one's views about abortion, the question of a woman's right to make decisions about her body is not a color-coded question.

Of course, given the nature of our double oppression it is often difficult to distinguish where racism ends and sexism begins. This we do know: They converge; and thus we cannot afford to fight inequality and oppression solely on one front. To draw an analogy, if both arms were tied behind your back as you prepared to swim, would you choose to have only one released? I trust not.

Hopefully more and more of us will in word and deed step up our efforts against sexism. As we do so we will surely be accused of being anti-men and we will be called man-bashers. Such accusations are not new. From academic works to everyday conversations, and from the days of slavery to the present moment we have heard these myths: "Black women were so busy taking care of themselves that they sold their men down the river"; "Every chance they got those slave women were in Massa's bed gettin' over"; "Black women had it easy in the Big House"; "Whenever there were a few jobs to be had, Black women would go and take them away from their men." Behold! The machete-wielding Black Matriarch, Mammy, and Jezebel rolled up in one.

There is indeed nothing new under the sun. Today in many Black communities this most cruel of myths about African American women is still being perpetuated, albeit modernized, updated, new and improved. This old myth took on new life in the late 1980s when African American women writers began to receive greater visibility. Some African American male writers viciously disparaged the works of African American women. They branded them anti-men and claimed that the only reason they were being published was because African American women were in cahoots with White men to degrade African American men. The most notorious example of such attacks was, of course, the condemnation of Alice Walker for "hanging out our dirty laundry" in *The Color Purple*. This kind of criticism is most disturbing because it seeks to stifle us and prevent us from talking about and thus ultimately dealing with our realities. Who could honestly deny that many of the incidents in that novel are as real as fiction can get? This is not to say that Alice Walker assumes that these were or are the experiences of every African American woman. They were not my personal experience; but because they were not, I do not assume they are no one's experience. Nor do I feel that truth, no matter how ugly, should be censored. Of course, not all African American men were of the same stripe. In *The Sexual Mountain and Black Women Writers: Adventures in Sex, Literature and Real Life,* Calvin Hernton, for one, sought to fulfill "the burning need for a black male writer to speak out against the red bricks of slander and bigotry that are hurled at black women and the literature they produce."[5] In his attempts to do just this, Hernton illustrated the negative portrayals of African American women in the literature of African American men as well as the fact that African American men have historically been the ordained and self-proclaimed lords of African American literature.

I make reference to this controversy not to reopen old wounds or instigate a resumption of hostilities, but rather to illustrate that like democracy, the realization of women's rights—the most basic of which is the right of self-expression—will be a noisy and messy affair. In all of this I would hope that men and women alike would realize that African American women cannot really oppress men, any more than African Americans can be racists. Women sometimes do express a blanket condemnation of men as African Americans sometimes do of White people (for example, "All men are dogs"; "All White people

[5] New York: Anchor Books/Doubleday, 1987.

are evil"). Such sweeping statements are, of course, defensive moves: efforts on the part of the exploited to defend their dignity by doing a wholesale attack on "the Other." But African American women do not have the *power* to truly bash African American men any more than African Americans have the *power* required to be racists, that is, to systematically deny White folks access to the good things in our world.

We African American women cannot afford to spend too much time looking over our shoulders for "red bricks of slander and bigotry." For there is a long stretch between what feminism is calling for and the realization of gender equality. The victory is not in asking to be treated equally, but in being treated equally.

In the 1960s in the context of the Civil Rights/ Black Liberation movement someone would say, "We know what we are against, but what are we for?" The same applies to the gender question. We women know we do not appreciate being dismissed as silly, or hysterical. We know we do not like being paid less money than men for doing the same work. And we surely know that we do not like being physically and sexually abused. It is therefore time we start focusing on what we want and asking: "What are we for? What is our vision? What kind of world do we want to live in?"

I look expectantly toward a day of new men and new women whose job opportunities and earning potential will not be based on the combination of their chromosomes, but on the content of their credentials. I want to live in a society where the dreams and aspirations of girls and boys will not be predetermined as they exit the womb. In this day of new women and new men people will have children not because to do so is some litmus test of woman- or manhood; rather, fully understanding the tremendous responsibility parenting involves, they genuinely want to have children. In such a day, just as "career women" will not be feared, resented, or viewed as unnatural, women who choose to be homemakers will not be berated, but fully recognized and appreciated as working women, too. At the same time, the needs and concerns of fathers who work outside the home will be addressed no less than those of mothers who do the same. Do I see marriage as we have traditionally known it in this new day? Yes and no.

Today, African American women must think about what they want in terms of intimate relationships in ways they never have before. This is a consequence of the crises that have taken their toll on our population of African American men, as well as wider social changes and the yearnings for greater fulfillment in the hearts and minds of women. As tradition's grip loosens bit by bit, African American women are considering and experiencing a range of alternatives to the familiar pattern of being married with children: from a fairly permanent state of singleness with occasional dating to lesbianism to "significant-othering" with African American and non–African American men. None of these lifestyles is new to the African American community. What is new, however, is their movement toward the center of acknowledgement and acceptance. It is therefore quite conceivable that even if the numbers of available African American men were to increase, African American women will continue to explore and exercise a range of options in terms of relationships. At the same time I do not believe marriage will or should go the way of the dinosaur.

In the past women entered marriage to varying degrees for economic security, social acceptability, and to have "legitimate" children. In this new era women will, I trust, marry for far more substantive and enduring reasons. In "the new order" of marriages I would hope that the realization of gender equality will not stop at an equitable division of household chores and equal (quality) input into the rearing of children if a couple has them, but will extend to an issue that has led many a marriage to founder. The issue is money.

Today and into the future there will be cases where a woman is no longer economically dependent on her husband and, in fact, her salary outstrips his. Now what is to be done? Will we be able to bring to that marriage the same notions of equality that women have sought for themselves in the past? We should. For if we bristle at the proposition that she is less than he because she earns less, how can we tolerate the idea that he is less than she because he earns less?

The same applies to the issue of status. For years women have been Mrs. So-and-So, and if a wife had a career it took a back seat to her husband's. In the future, as now, while the man may or may not earn the most money, the woman may have the higher status and her career in some respects may take priority over his. Such cases are not as rare as they once were, but they still take place in uncharted territory. What does it mean, for example, that I am the president of Spelman College and my husband is the First Man? There are books, articles, and a good deal of folklore about First Ladies. But what about First Men? We do not have rules, language, or protocol for this turn of events. This became glaringly apparent during my visit to Japan. At a dinner which followed a lecture I had given, a man asked my husband about the kind of work he did and inquired whether my husband was giving lectures during our visit. My husband replied, "No," and proceeded to explain that he was there to accompany and support his wife. A veil of disbelief and astonishment befell the man's face. Then, as if a light bulb flashed on, he said, "Oh, I see! You are her manager." He had to find an old role because he could not believe a new one. Hopefully in the future we will not be preoccupied with roles that are exclusively identified with women or men.

If you are a feminist you have to imagine a lot more marriages where the woman earns more money than the man or has more public prominence, or both. As well, there will be instances where the earnings and status will be on a par. In any case, you have to imagine the development of new ways of being woman and man whereby identity and esteem are not bound up in a paycheck or a professional title. In this new day, women and men will of course open doors for each other and a seat will be relinquished to whomever is wearier. I also look forward to a day when women will not have to be unnecessarily self-conscious about their actions and monitor those of men.

This brings to mind an evening when I was getting ready for a dinner of a corporate Board of Directors on which I am the only female. As I flipped through my closet I thought, "Should I wear a suit to look more like them, or a dress to suit my mood?" At the dinner, as the men talked and talked about sports I wondered, "Should I join in the conversation to show that I, a woman, can be 'one of the boys' or should I remain conspicuously silent almost 'in defense' of my gender?" In this new society I trust I will not have to clutter my head with such trivial questions or organize my behavior in response to men. Usually, what to wear or talk about when in the company of men is the least of my problems, but I offer this incident to illustrate the frustrations women sometimes endure and the headtrips we often go through in proving that we are not "just a woman." As we all know, it's frustrating and pointless to try to prove a negative. When such mental energy need no longer be exerted on trying to do so, it will be a welcome sign that systemic sexism is in trouble.

As with the struggle against racism, if we are ever to make sexism a thing of the past, we must give our dreams and visions more than lip service. Expressions of inequality are nurtured and socially reproduced in two settings—the private and the public sphere—and we must struggle against them in both arenas.

That struggle must involve confronting the reality that men are not the only ones who perpetuate sexism and encourage gender inequality. In our discussions of sexism we tend to focus solely on what men are or are not doing and overlook our participation in our oppression. For example, we put ourselves in gender straitjackets when we use sex and sexuality as the exclusive way of defining ourselves. Result? Instead of gender being a healthy, liberating attribute, it becomes a constraint. Likewise, we entrap ourselves in sexist notions and behavior when we proclaim: "I am in charge of the kitchen," or "I am the one who takes care of the babies." It is we womenfolk who color-code our children—pink for girls, blue for boys—and perpetuate, no less than men, the trucks-for-boys and dolls-for-girls syndrome. We are quick to dissuade girl-children from playing with action figures and may even chastise and ridicule a boy-child who wants to play "tea party." And let us not forget that it is we women, along with men, who make comments such as: "Look at Mommy's little man, look how strong he is," as opposed to "Isn't she beautiful?" And who is it that assigns household tasks to daughters while excusing sons to go out for a game of touch football? As well, I'm sure most of you can recall a large family gathering where the women did all the cooking, most of the serving, and when all was said and eaten, the bulk of the cleaning up, too. Just imagine a five- or six-year-old boy or girl observing that scene. If it is a recurrent one will he or she not grow up with fixed ideas about men's versus women's work?

Clearly, we have a lot of help in tightening the gender straitjackets. The process begins early: from the strong slap on the buttocks of boy babies as opposed to the gentler one doctors give girl infants as they exit the womb. When it comes to our abilities, the gender straitjacket is tightened each time a teacher calls on the boys for answers to complex questions, ignoring the girls. The limited competency of women is implied by the profusion of heroes in literature and the paucity of sheroes, by the predominance of quotations and photographs of male experts and leaders in the media's coverage of major events and issues. Many song lyrics and poses in advertisements subtly and sometimes not so subtly promote the idea of women as sex objects. All of this helps to bind us into unhealthy images of women *and* men. When we see these images being perpetuated it is our responsibility to call the perpetrators on it.

One of the calls we need to make concerns one of the most basic features of human existence: Language. I know that gender equality will not be achieved solely or more rapidly by changes in language, but at the same time I know that language is not an insignificant matter. Indeed, it often expresses and thereby reinforces notions of inequality. For example, in social and professional settings alike many men think nothing of addressing a woman as "Sweetheart." The term itself is a perfectly appreciated one; but on the lips of someone with whom you do not have an intimate relationship it is disrespectful. There is an assumption that you are a "thing" as opposed to another human being and that a certain familiarity regardless of your rank and station is not inappropriate. Put another way, how often have you heard a man who is not on intimate terms with another man refer to him as "Sweetheart"? Rather than lecture men on this point, when one says, "Well, hello, sweetheart," I have adopted the policy of simply responding, "Well, sweetheart, how are you?"

When I first came to Spelman, whenever I heard

people refer to a Spelman student as a girl I called them on it, particularly in settings where reference was made to Morehouse men but Spelman girls. Our Vice-President and Dean of Student Affairs, who has a wonderful sense of humor, joined in the crusade and advanced it threefold. She put a "Woman Jar" in her office and any and every time someone—female or male—referred to a Spelman student as a girl, they had to put money in the jar. This "Woman Jar" was once quite full and would be emptied occasionally for a good cause, but in time it became less and less full until it was no longer needed.

Of course some will argue that "girl" is a harmless term of endearment, but in fact to refer to a woman as a girl is to reduce her to less than adult status. One would expect that African American men would especially understand a woman's sensitivity and objection to being called a girl given the bitter association they have with the habit of White people calling grown Black men boys. Again, language is not the end-all in gender relations, but being careful with it is a start, because what we say mirrors our conscious and unconscious attitudes.

To be a feminist one need not be a card-carrying member of one, two, or ten women's rights organizations. However, if one wishes to at least keep abreast of women's issues and keep track of the progress toward gender equality one needs to be aware of these organizations and in some way, however tangentially, plugged into them (if only to be on their mailing lists or have a subscription to their newsletters). To be certain, such groups and organizations can use all the womanpower they can get. Those among us who have the "joining disposition" should not go out scattershot and become a member of ten organizations. It makes far more sense to identify those groups that address issues—domestic violence, rape, sexual harassment on the job, child care, pay equity, employment discrimination, pornography, abortion—that are of prime interest to you, and then, of course to lend a helping hand. Some of us will stuff envelopes; some will woman hot lines. Still others will attend protest rallies and marches, organize seminars, teach courses, raise funds. And all will be contributing to the welfare and betterment of ourselves and our sisters.

I am not convinced that the coming of age of African American women into feminism can be achieved by switching terms, and I certainly see no reason that "feminism" or "feminist" should belong exclusively to White women. Yet, when Alice Walker coined the term "Womanist," many of us were attracted to it. We liked the sound, the feel of "Womanist." It struck a chord; it was familiar. Familiar because we remember our mothers, grandmothers, aunts, and other womenfolk pulling our pigtails and chiding us with "Don't come 'round here with those womanly ways of yours," or "You acting too womanish for me."

The word *Womanist* is more than a cozy stop down memory lane. We embrace it not only for its familiarity, but for its substance as well. The word contains a dynamism and a motive force. In her collection of essays, *In Search of Our Mothers' Gardens: Womanist Prose,* Walker defined womanist as "outrageous, audacious, courageous, or *willful* behavior," and, "committed to survival and wholeness of entire people, male *and* female."[6]

Walker went on to capture the reality that there are differences between the experiences of African American women and White women when she wrote: "Womanist is to feminist as purple is to lavender." With this wonderful phrase Alice Walker has made it clear that all women are at the same end of the color chart, that our experiences as women are not so different she need refer to radically different colors. Womanist is to feminist not as purple is to yellow, but as purple to lavender. A different hue of the same color.

In considering the statement one cannot ignore the obvious intensity of purple in comparison with lavender. The passion of purple does not detract from the legitimacy of lavender, but it does speak to the intensity of our oppression as African Americans and as women. As well, I hope it will speak to the intensity of our determination to be rid of oppression and the campaign we are potentially capable of waging against it.

Doing so will, to a large extent, require charting our own course toward gender equality based on our own concerns and approaches. Just as the problem with a woman standing behind her man is that she can't see where she's going, standing behind a woman of a different hue may confuse you about the best path for you to take.

If African American women are able to work in conjunction with other women of color and White women on mutual and separate agenda, there will

[6] San Diego: Harcourt Brace Jovanovich, 1983.

be more power to the movement. But if in some
instances such coalitions are not feasible or productive for African American women, then there may
have to be a temporary parting of the ways. Should
this occur we may be accused of splintering the
movement, of diluting its potency. There may arise
mutterings that we are being "too Black" or "getting
Black all of a sudden." We of course will know that
we have been Black for a *very* long time. And once
again, we must keep on keepin' on, strengthened by
the truth in Anna Julia Cooper's oft-quoted declara-
tion:

> Only the Black Woman can say, "when and where I
> enter, in the quiet, undisputed dignity of my wom-
> anhood, without violence and without suing or special
> patronage, then and there the whole . . . *race enters
> with me.*"[7]

More than anything else, African American
women who are feminists and mothers or guardians
must find ways to raise their girls and their boys as
feminists, too. We are the individuals with the greatest power to raise a generation of new women and
new men.

[7] *A Voice from the South* (Xenia, Ohio: Aldine Printing House, 1892).

# Let's Do Windows
on the World

*But I am not tragically colored. There is no great sorrow dammed up in my soul, nor lurking behind my eyes. I do not mind at all. I do not belong to the sobbing school of Negrohood who hold that nature somehow has given them a lowdown dirty deal and whose feelings are hurt about it. . . . No, I do not weep at the world—I am too busy sharpening my oyster knife.*

    —ZORA NEALE HURSTON, "How It Feels to Be Colored Me" (1928), reprinted in *I Love Myself When I Am Laughing . . . And Then Again When I Am Looking Mean and Impressive: A Zora Neale Hurston Reader,* edited by Alice Walker (1979).

WHEN WE THINK of oppression, we generally think in terms of the opportunities and life chances it robs its victims of; and rightly so, since this is the most immediate and obvious sting. In the long run, however, the real horror of oppression is that it can rob people of their will to try, and make them take themselves out of the running of life.

Racism, sexism, or any form or system of oppression is abuse, plain and simple. And abuse is a great paralyzer. If persistent and pervasive enough it whittles away at the soul. It numbs the spirit. It stifles and sometimes utterly destroys an openness and an adventuresome posture toward the world and its wonders.

The blows of racism and sexism have been so severe as to plunge many African American women into a place so far down that, as the saying goes, they have to reach up to touch bottom. There are those, of course, who have had far fewer misfortunes. Yet, here we find that despite whatever material advantages they were born into or themselves acquired, the bombardment of blatant and subliminal negative messages about who they are has seduced many a woman into shutting herself up in a cramped, poorly lighted room with no view. Such a woman is cut off from the world and ultimately from herself.

Writer, folklorist, and anthropologist Zora Neale Hurston was a complicated and contradictory character. Tucked inside her marvelous one-liner "No, I do not weep at the world—I am too busy sharpening my oyster knife," is that streak of individualism that was, for all her brilliance, part of Hurston's personality. By individualism I do not mean a healthy sense of independence and self-reliance, but that level of self-centeredness that can keep you so absorbed in your needs, so busy stockpiling your pearls that you fail to see, let alone tend to, the needs of those in the world around you.

What I like about the phrase, however, is the way in which it underlines one's own power. It is as if zany, erratic, lovable ole Zora is wagging her finger at her folk and saying, "Don't just sit there sobbing over your predicament! You can be an agent of change! You can alter your situation!" She is serving a strong reminder to each of her sisters that just because others perceive you as a second-class citizen, you don't have to act like one. Hurston's statement can also be seen as an indictment against something that, while not particular to African American women, is nonetheless unfortunate and counterproductive to the movement for freedom and equality. Namely: provincialism.

This provincialism manifests itself in a myriad of ways. One of which is in our resistance to recognizing and embracing diversity among ourselves. It is as if the propaganda others peddle that seeks to define and categorize us has seeped into our consciousness and beguiled us into typecasting ourselves. It is as if we, too, have bought into the idea that there is some such phenomenon as *The* Black Woman—when nothing is farther from the truth!

African American women are as arrayed across the class spectrum as variably we are across the nation's terrain. We are highly educated and we are illiterate. Some of us do not work outside the home because we've chosen not to, some of us, because we are unable to. Professionally, we are marine biologists, accountants, psychologists, florists, housekeepers, veterinarians, secretaries, architects. Our interests and activities extend beyond partying, gossiping, and frying chicken (although some of us do that, too), and include skiing, stamp collecting, gardening, swimming, volunteer work, reading, bowling. Some of us have been coddled and overindulged throughout our lives; some of us have been physically, emotionally, and sexually abused; and still others of us have experienced neither the former nor the latter. We are heterosexual, homosexual, bisexual, and asexual. We marry within the race, we marry outside the race, and some of us don't marry at all. We are divorced, separated, and widowed. Many of us have children (all of whom, I hope, we consider *very* legitimate) and some of us do not. African American women are represented in every belief system: Some of us follow Christ, others the teachings of Buddha. Some of us look to the Koran, others to the Torah. We are deists and atheists. Politically, we run the gamut from socialists and Communists to liberals, conservatives, and even nothing-ists. Some of our lives are characterized by activism, others by apathy. Clearly, as I have so often said, if you've seen one of us you *ain't* seen us all!

Yes, there are ties that bind us one to another, but they do not and should not restrain us from being ourselves. On one level we are aware of our diversity; so evident is it in our outer selves. The most conspicuous dimension of our diversity is our skin tones and body types. And it goes without saying that we can and will do almost everything imaginable to our hair: crimp it, dreadlock it, straighten it, dye it, braid it. When it comes to such externals we reveal and acknowledge our diversity, but when it comes to the real fabric of our lives—political views, sexual preference, talents, interests—often we cannot imagine its existence. If confronted with the evidence we sometimes pretend it isn't there. Or worse, we ridicule and censure it.

Far too many of us assume that African Americans have only one party: Democratic. When we discover a Republican, a Communist, or a Libertarian we are dumbstruck. Many presume that every African American woman is a Christian or at least believes in God. Then up speaks an agnostic or an atheist and we fall silent and wary. Upon encountering an African American woman who is studying Russian, Chinese, or Sanskrit for that matter, some of us no less than White folk, react as if that woman were an aberration, or worse, "trying to be White." And is it actually the strangest thing in the world for an African American woman to have a passion for Vivaldi, Liszt, or Gershwin? Must she only love Duke Ellington and Ella Fitzgerald, Anita Baker and Stevie Wonder?

Indeed, this inability to recognize how very different we are in our tastes, interests, and perspectives is in part a consequence of stereotypes perpetuated about us. But it is also a by-product of that sense of solidarity so vital to our survival and which to varying degrees has at times called for and practically demanded uniformity. Here is a case in point. During the height of the Black-consciousness movement when activists rallied African American women to stop straightening their hair, the Afro became a badge. It served an important purpose, but became a bone of contention and divisive when some interpreted the Afro as *the* barometer of a person's consciousness. The anthropologist in me observes that today, during a period when African American women are exploring a wider range of pursuits, political affiliations, and lifestyles than ever before, they are also sporting a wider range of hairstyles than ever before. With that said, I will leave the subject of Hair as Metaphor alone.

Our limited vision of ourselves is expressed in assumptions African American women of one socioeconomic group make about those of another. Many middle-income women fail to recognize diversity among women on public assistance and those who swell the ranks of the working poor, and in so doing, join the chorus of those who speak in stereotypes. Just as surely as we should cease to be shocked to encounter an African American woman who is a neurosurgeon or jazz bassist, we should not be puzzled to discover a factory worker who writes poetry or is a member of a Shakespearean theatrical company; nor should we be surprised to encounter an African American woman who lives in a housing project who speaks standard American English very well.

For certain, our collective experience in America has been characterized by *de jure* and *de facto* prohibition from entering certain professions and pursuing a range of endeavors and interests. As a result, many of us have come to accept the fact that African Americans simply did not do certain things and dream certain dreams. We allow the reality of what we did not do to negate the possibilities of what we surely can accomplish.

An activist once told me of a revealing episode during his travels in Africa in the 1960s. He set the stage by recounting how he had been speaking out boldly about the potential of Black folk. Indeed, he argued, if simply given a chance, there is nothing that Black people can't do. There he was, a Black Power advocate par excellence. However, when he boarded a plane and discovered that the pilot was Black, he said to himself, "Oh, God. How's he going to know how to fly this plane? I'm in trouble now." I shudder to think how he might have reacted had the pilot been not only Black but a woman. We may chuckle at that story, but I would venture to guess that it is nervous laughter because it reminds us of instances when we have had similar reactions, of times when because of years and years of propaganda about Black inferiority we have doubted the competency of an African American physician, accountant, attorney, or other professional. Many would argue that their suspicions were grounded in the fact that African Americans often received inferior training. This assumption of course goes hand in hand with the assumption that White people received superior training. Neither assumption holds water, and even in cases where Whites were privileged to have access to superior training, it does not necessarily follow that they would turn out competent.

Failure to acknowledge and respect diversity is the basis of racism, sexism, and a host of other insidious and infamous "isms." A perception of singularity is often expressed in such deplorable generalities as

"Black people are lazy"; "Jews are money-hungry"; "Indians are alcoholics"; "Puerto Ricans are all on welfare"; "White people are devils." While we may not use the term "bigotry" when a racial or ethnic group fails to acknowledge diversity within its own ranks, that is exactly what it is. We African American women know bigotry all too well. How dare we perpetuate it, especially one toward another.

Accepting our diversity is not just humane. It is exhilarating. Although there is a way in which each of us never ceases to be an African American and a woman, to be in the presence of an African American woman painted in a different way is on the most basic level an opportunity for learning. And learning leads to growth. As well, even if you find yourself in the presence of a woman who is politically more to the right or left than you, or pro what you are anti, it is a dazzling reminder that we, too, come in many colors and forms, and it is an affirmation of our humanity, something which others have long labored to deny us.

Championing and looking expectantly for diversity among us will not in and of itself make us free, but it is a step in the right direction. On a more immediate level it will encourage and stimulate each of us to do a little stretching out when it comes to our individual horizons. Here, too, we find a degree of provincialism, as reflected in what we read, watch, listen to, and engage ourselves in. For example, I know many African American women who can well afford it but have never been outside the city in which they live. Of course this is not peculiar to us. Many an Italian woman who lived on my block in Brooklyn had never been to Manhattan.

One does not have to prefer European classical music over Black classical music—otherwise known as jazz. But part of living in the world as a well-rounded person is to know at least *something* of various styles of music. Similarly, everything in a museum is not dry, boring, and alien to who we are. Yet, in museum after museum we are noticeably few, and often appallingly so in those that feature African and African American art. Likewise, just as we are few and far between at symphony halls, neither do we pack the halls for a jazz concert.

If for some, money is a restraining force, in many cases money is not the issue. Any woman who is able to buy a VCR, a new car, Chanel No. 5, Chivas Regal, or gold earrings can afford a two- or three-dollar admission fee to a museum, or twenty, thirty or even fifty dollars for theater tickets. And what is the excuse when the events are free? It is simply a function of choices and initiatives.

A woman who taught at a junior college with a predominantly African American student body told me of the time she planned an excursion for one of her classes: a visit to an African American art museum. At the outset her students were decidedly uninterested. Their position was that art was not relevant to their lives. But after they experienced the work of Benny Andrews and others in the exhibit, they were transfixed and transformed, and more than a few of them planned to tell their friends and visit the museum again. Most amazing of all is that the museum was across the street from the building in which the college was housed and the majority of the students were unaware of its existence.

This incident is surely not an isolated one. In such

scenarios our initial response might be to fault the students for being unobservant and initially so close-minded about art. But in truth we must all shoulder some of the blame, including our cultural institutions, which are negligent when it comes to aggressively making their presence known to the range of people in the surrounding communities; and our educators, who are either too lazy or unimaginative to engage in creative pedagogy and take students—even if kicking and screaming—to other heights.

This is not to suggest that every African American woman should reorganize her life to become a constant theatergoer and museum patron; but it is to suggest that a lifestyle of limited exposure is a strong guarantee of cramped and narrow dreams and aspirations, which in turn lead to a kind of self-imposed isolation.

This self-imposed isolation is also evident in a lack of interest and participation in the political and social issues that swirl and sometimes rage around us. Indifference to what goes on in our nation at large is expressed in comments such as "Why should I care about the deficit? I don't have anything to do with that." One of the most damaging examples was when AIDS first entered our vocabularies and many African Americans made the offhand assessment that it was a "White peoples' disease" and therefore *their* problem (just as, I might add, many White heterosexuals shrugged it off as a homosexual disease and therefore *their* problem). As we all now know, AIDS is everybody's problem.

Obviously our reluctance or failure to be involved is not a matter of some genetic or chromosomal predisposition. To a large extent a deep involvement in matters of the world has been systematically denied many of us. In essence, our apathy has been conditioned. African American women have not been among the power brokers in our nation. In fact, we have been subjected to double-barreled programming to stay out of the nation's business. On the one hand, African Americans were told in words and deeds that the business of the nation was the business of White folk (the most obvious example was the fight we had to wage for the vote). On the other hand, women have long been projected as nonthinking, nonpolitical creatures.

This failure to be informed and involved is also on some level a result of a disenchantment many African Americans feel with the political process and a distrust of politicians. But, of course, standing aside from electoral politics is hardly the way to make it work.

Our educational system has also played a role in encouraging apathy among some of its citizenry. For instance, I seriously doubt that children in most inner-city classrooms are being taught a range of important world issues. And the significance of these issues to our youngsters receives even less attention.

Some will cry battle fatigue from the blows of racism and sexism as an excuse for not being more informed and involved. I can almost hear a sister say, "I'm being messed with every which way I turn and you're asking me to do something else that isn't going to feed my child or help me get that promotion?" My response is, "Yes," because such an attitude is a putdown to our intelligence and the relevance of our opinions. More important, it is a setback because given the oppression African American women experience, we can least afford to sit on the sidelines when it comes to political, social, and economic issues.

The times demand that we come to understand the interconnectedness between the "Big Issues" and our lives. We need to understand the drug scourge in terms of political and economic forces far beyond our inner-city communities. Of course we must organize to rid our neighborhoods of individual drug dealers, but we must also understand that drugs are connected with national and international politics and economics. The drug pusher on the corner does not have the means to transport narcotics into the country, bribe customs officials, or launder massive amounts of drug money. Likewise, we must understand that health care is big business with its eye on the bottom line; and subsequently, unless more people join the campaign for affordable if not universal health care in our country, the hospital emergency room will continue to be a place where millions of poor African American women and their children spend the day when they are ill or injured because they do not have premier medical coverage, if they have any at all.

An African American woman may be correct when she declares that she has nothing to do with the budget deficit. However, she should bear in mind that the deficit has a lot to do with her if she is at all dependent upon or in need of social services. After all, when the budget crunch comes and cutting must be done, the choice that is most often made is to cut in those social service areas which the poor, people of color, and women need the most.

Perhaps the single most frightening expression of

African American women's disassociation from politics and the starkest example of our need to get involved is the issue of war and peace. First of all, although the armed services are not composed exclusively of men, the business of war and the actual mechanics of carrying it out is still largely men's work. This is not to say however that it is their business alone. Who are the "men at war" if not our sons, brothers, nephews, husbands, and friends? Nor should we forget that if the bomb is dropped it will not be color- or gender-coded. Furthermore, if we look at the issue of peace in the context of our struggle, how can we be uninterested in this issue when an America at peace is necessary if we are going to address the wretched problems that plague and confront us at home. When there is trouble abroad, even our most pressing domestic issues are put on hold.

I am reminded of the anecdote where the professor asks, "What is the greatest threat to American democracy—ignorance or apathy?" to which a truculent student responds, "I don't know and I don't care." African Americans cannot afford not to know and not to care about the major issues of our day. To do so is to acquiesce to the status quo, if not to threaten our survival. Moreover, if the ceiling of your rented apartment falls in, it is not just the landlord's problem. This is to say that although there are aspects of our nation that have not been citizen-friendly to African Americans, this is, after all where we live. This is our country as much as anyone else's and we have the right and responsibility to mind its business.

As we move beyond our backgrounds, our neighborhoods, our racial and ethnic communities and come to know ourselves and our nation better, we must no less reach out and know the world.

In the summer of 1985, in Nairobi, Kenya, there was a gathering of womenfolk of the world. Young women, old women, women of every hue, women of various religions, women of every political view, gathered together for the End of the Decade International Women's Conference. Although I did not attend the conference, I have relished stories about what it was like, and I have thought over and over again about a phrase that became the slogan of that conference: Think Globally and Act Locally!

The term "global village" has become a standard in our vocabulary. We have a sense, of course, of our shrinking world. We know that we can fly to Ouagadougou in Burkina Faso, and that fax machines, televisions, and computers can instantly put us in touch with people around the world. Indeed, events that occur in our tomorrow in one part of the world become the subject of our nightly news.

We are aware, too, of our reliance on other people and countries for necessary—and, yes, unnecessary —things. Dr. Martin Luther King, Jr., reminded us that we are all interdependent.

> Every nation is an heir of a vast treasury of ideas and labor to which both the living and the dead of all nations have contributed. Whether we realize it or not, each of us lives eternally "in the red." We are everlasting debtors to known and unknown men and women. When we arise in the morning, we go into the bathroom where we reach for a sponge which is provided for us by a Pacific Islander. We reach for soap that is created for us by a European. Then at the table, we

drink coffee which is provided for us by a South American, or tea by a Chinese, or cocoa by a West African. Before we leave for our jobs we are already beholden to more than half the world.[1]

Of course, thinking globally must be far more profound than knowing that your car was made in Germany and your shoes in Brazil. It is a keen awareness that there is a world community, and as a citizen of the world, for better or for worse, your life and life circumstances are connected to and affected by that of your fellow citizens of this planet. However, like many Americans the majority of us do not keep up with current events in nations around the world. We are forced into awareness about what is going on in Lithuania, Haiti, Liberia, or India when a major crisis or event becomes front-page news. Often, however, our attention span does not last long enough for the follow-up stories that appear on the back page once the media determine the subject no longer merits first-page attention. Even when we begin to follow a particular event we may give up caring because "it gets so complicated." Like many other Americans, we are, for example, hard-pressed to distinguish between Nicaragua and El Salvador. Even if we do read the captions on photographs, begin to keep track of an event, or vaguely know where a country is on the map, we are uninterested in the "little details" of it all. Result? We, too, think that the official language of Brazil is Spanish.

Even if you take the position that you are only interested in those who "look like you," there are a

[1] *Where Do We Go from Here: Chaos or Community?* (New York: Harper & Row, 1967).

whole lot of women in the world—in Africa, Latin America, the Caribbean, Canada, the Pacific Islands, Asia, and Europe—who look like you. But here, too, by and large we are ignorant of the lives and situations of our own folk around the world. Some of us use "West Indian" and "Jamaican" interchangeably. We think there are no metropolises in sub-Saharan Africa. We cannot imagine that there are Black people in Britain. To be totally unaware of a large, vibrant, and oppressed Black community in London is not good for us, or the folks of Black Britannia. This absence of understanding and knowledge about people of African descent around the world is reflected in that classic tension between Black folks whose roots run deep in the United States and those whose more recent ancestry is in the Caribbean. And lest we forget, such ignorance of other people of the world is not limited to low-income or unschooled people. Too often African American college students look upon students from Somalia, Bermuda, or South Africa, as "foreign" people.

As we enter the next century we will be out of the running before it starts if we have not learned to think, speak, and move beyond the borders imposed upon us by birth. Just as with European Americans, much of our history and culture is tied to places outside America. But far less often than European Americans, we do not consciously study, learn about, and visit "whence we come." This is to say that while we owe it to ourselves to know the world, we have a special responsibility to know about Africa and African-based cultures around the world.

We cannot fully understand ourselves and the events that surround us unless we think beyond our own life, our own neighborhood, our own nation. As we anthropologists say: "It's scarcely the fish who discovers water!" You must get outside that water to truly see and understand it. Otherwise, "the water" around you becomes so habitual, so ordinary, so necessary for your life that you never intellectually or emotionally confront it. Consider how many of our leaders truly soared after they had experienced the realities of other people and cultures. When Malcolm X went to the Middle East, when Dr. Martin Luther King, Jr., discovered the philosophy of Mahatma Gandhi something great happened for African Americans. Malcolm X's concern with the plight of Black people in America was informed by his experiences in the Arab world, and consequently he became far more of an internationalist in his views. King was strongly influenced by Gandhi and went on to develop a particular philosophy of social change through nonviolence that greatly influenced the American Civil Rights movement.

To exist in a vacuum, to live with the absence of comparative information about the lives of others and ourselves means we will not only continue to perpetuate stereotypes about other people, we will do the same of ourselves. Learning about the lives of other people is enriching because we come to understand their reality. But the major enriching quality of learning about the lives of others is that it allows you a different, enhanced perspective on yourself and your circumstances—one that only comes when you are distanced from yourself. In other words, although going into the world and seeing things may not solve your problem, it may well improve your analysis.

pleasures of being a tourist, to take in all the tourist traps that you know to be tourist traps—but they are fun anyway. However, at some point one needs to go beyond "touristing" and particularly that five-cities-in-five-days whirlwind that is such a part of the American way of travel. At some point we need to give up those all-inclusive packages to the Caribbean where your hotel complex is an island unto itself and your jaunts outside the hotel grounds are prearranged and nicely orchestrated, so as to minimize and control your contact with "the natives." (That is in some sense tantamount to going to someone's home for dinner, bringing your food with you, and eating alone in the most comfortable corner you can find. Where is the experience?)

If you have been to Jamaica once before, on your second visit, skip the normal tourist fare (after all, if you've seen one fireater and "crabman" you've seen them all). Take a side trip to visit a Maroon community and feel the still palpable legacy of Africans who defied European slave owners. Rather than go "Yankin'," why not get acquainted with everyday folk to find out what life is like for those who live there as opposed to those who merely visit. While doing this may be especially meaningful to us in places of the Pan-African world, it is no less a better way to be a traveler if you are in Australia, Hawaii, Ireland, or Montana for that matter (if you're from Montana, then substitute with New Mexico).

True travel is in some sense a history lesson and a learning experience about the here and now. Just because you are on vacation does not mean you have to be on vacation from life. Everyone who travels often has her favorite place, but often like our fellow

Americans we go to the same place again and again (and again) not out of a burning desire to really get to know a particular city or country, but because of a lack of imagination and curiosity. Then, too, some of us assert that African Americans simply do not go certain places. Why not? Is it that we are afraid we might not be made to feel welcomed or made comfortable? Well, do you always feel welcomed and comfortable in America?

I am reminded of a story a freelance writer once told me in connection with what she thought to be a fascinating trip to Iceland. Upon her return she was eager to do a travel story on it, and in particular for an African American–interest magazine for which she occasionally wrote. The story idea was rejected because as one editor explained, "Black people don't go to Iceland." African Americans do, and should go anywhere in the world.

I realize that not everyone is financially able to travel, or at least not as often as we would like. Fortunately, there are alternative vehicles, the most obvious of which are books, certainly about the Greece of Aristotle and the Britain of Churchill, but also about the India of Gandhi, the Mexico of Zapata, and the America of Mary McLeod Bethune.

Books are not the only means to bring the world to us and us to the world. A student who may not be able to travel can learn to think globally by actively seeking out speakers and cultural groups to come to her campus. A church congregation can do likewise. We can visit other lands by listening to public radio, watching public television, taking in foreign films, and reading magazines that feature the world as well as America. You can meet the world by attending lecture series at museums and other institutions and organizations featuring discussions about the history and culture of all the nations on our planet. Within the borders of the United States there are people from every part of the world speaking languages from nearly every language group, and practicing beliefs and rituals of incredible diversity. You can get to know these people and their culture often without traveling very far at all.

Meeting the world is not just a joyride and source of personal insight and enlightenment. As we reach out and acquaint ourselves with the world, we will not only think globally but, hopefully, feel globally as well. Thinking globally will instill in us the capacity for empathy—that honest concern for others that sees the connections between the yearning for freedom and equality in an East German in Leipzig, a South African in Johannesburg, and an African American in Atlanta; that sees the ties that bind a physician in a small African village, a nurse in the hills above Port-au-Prince, and a doctor in rural Mississippi. As it increasingly registers that we are all of the same human species, we will come to know that a homeless child in Palestine is no less deserving of our prayers and concern than a homeless child in Harlem.

As more and more African American women reach outside the limitations set upon us, we will truly begin to see ourselves more clearly. We will see that while we are one, we are also many and diverse; and because we are we have much to share with one another. We will discover, too, that we have much to give to the world and the world has much to offer us. Yes, my sisters, the world belongs to us, too. To all of us. The stereotype of Black folks caring only about the race question and women being incapable of taking on the complexities of politics, economics, and international affairs falls on us African American women as a double myth. Let us not present ourselves as "proof" of these stereotypes.

"No," an African American woman proclaims, "I don't do windows."

That is all well and good. But, my sister, do begin to do windows on the world. It will be good for your mind and your soul—and it'll be good for the world, too.

# Sturdy Black Bridges

*"I" cannot reach fulfillment without "thou." The self cannot be self without other selves. Self-concern without other-concern is like a tributary that has no outward flow to the ocean. Stagnant, still, and stale, it lacks both life and freshness.*

   —Dr. Martin Luther King, Jr., *Where Do We Go From Here: Chaos or Community?* (1967)

*To die for the revolution is a one-shot deal; to live for the revolution means taking on the more difficult commitment of changing our day-to-day life patterns.*

   —Frances M. Beal, "Double Jeopardy: To Be Black and Female" (1969), reprinted in *Sisterhood Is Powerful: An Anthology of Writings from the Women's Liberation Movement,* edited by Robin Morgan (1970)

AS YOU OPEN UP and out to the world, as you grow in awareness and empathy for human beings in nations near and far, you may see more acutely, or perhaps anew, the condition of those in your own backyard. This revelation, no matter how great or small, should not be an end in itself. It should not stop as a static exercise in collecting comparative data, but serve as a catalyst to your becoming an agent of change. It should bring to your remembrance the second part of the slogan from the women's conference in Nairobi: the imperative to "Act Locally."

Why?

Because charity begins at home. This is not to suggest that charity should *remain* at home. On the contrary, it is often only after you have taken care of business on the home front that you can most effectively take on matters outside the home. Malcolm X often suggested that we would never change South Africa until we changed Mississippi. Malcolm X truly had a way with words when it came to capturing multifaceted truths. In the 1950s and 1960s Mississippi symbolized White oppression in its vilest form, and Black deprivation and degradation at its worst. To be sure, America could never sincerely or in good conscience bring real pressure to bear on the South African government to end apartheid until America cleaned up its backyard and rooted out its version of apartheid, Jim Crow. Moreover, a stronger, healthier Black America, a people that has moved out of "Mississippi," will prove a fiercer, more effective ally to the oppressed in South Africa.

Today, Mississippi is certainly not what it used to be, but Black America is not what it should be. In cities across the country there are African Americans still living in "Mississippi." Systemic oppression and deprivation have yielded bumper crops of crime, violence, substance abuse, homelessness, under- and unemployment, health crises, illiteracy, and the worst enemy to the soul: Despair.

Black America is in need of charity.

When we think of charity we often think of spectacular benefit concerts and $500-a-plate dinners where the wealthy rise to the occasion to avert a crisis or support a worthy cause. Charity brings to mind images of children toting canned goods to school around Thanksgiving to be distributed among the poor, who may then slip through the cracks of their consciousness until next Thanksgiving rolls around. As well, our minds might flash back to scenes of people full of holiday cheer leaving department stores heavy-laden with packages, but thoughtful enough to toss some spare change into Salvation Santa's kettle.

I am not belittling any of the above; but such images do not do justice to the kind of charity Black America needs. The kind of charity I am talking about is not a seasonal or annual event, but it is captured in the true meaning of the word *charity:* Love. This is not the dreamy-eyed state of mind and emotions most associated with the first bloom of romantic love, but the love that sees a need and rolls up its sleeves and expresses itself through action. This kind of love enables you to reach out to those you may not personally know, or even particularly like. This kind of love recognizes that we are all part of the same circle: the living, the dead, and the yet unborn.

I do not mean this only in the sense of African cosmology, but in very real and concrete terms. For if we consider the state of Black America, "the living" becomes a metaphor for the more able and fortunate among us; "the dead," those whose potential has been almost if not utterly destroyed; the "yet unborn," the children poised between the two, and whose fate will in large measure be determined by the scope and substance of the charity the "living" extend today.

Do you, an African American, love African Americans?

The question is not do you like all African Americans; nor is it are you always pleased and approving of what every African American does. These are questions I am certain few could answer in the affirmative. There are times when we cringe at what some African Americans do: when a group of young people commit heinous acts; when a so-called leader goes before the world supposedly on our behalf and makes a public spectacle of him- or herself. Yes, there are times when we cringe and are embarrassed by our people, and for a split second we may even feel ashamed of ourselves—just for being Black. We've already talked about why: When one of us soars we all feel ready to take flight; and when one of us makes a serious mistake, we fear we might all have to pay the price.

The idea is not to embrace all African Americans

as a matter of course, but to treasure our culture, our spirit, our intrinsic worth as human beings. In this sense, do you love your people? The living? The dead? The yet unborn?

If your response is a soul-searched "No," then that ole demon racism can claim another clear and decisive victory. To those who respond in the affirmative, then I have to ask: If you love yourself and your people, what are you prepared to do to ensure our survival? Are you prepared to roll up your sleeves?

The problems confronting African Americans are multiple and intense[1]:

- African American females—12.7% of the U.S. female population—account for 53% of U.S. female AIDS cases.
- 1 in every 2 of us receives inadequate prenatal care.
- The maternal mortality rate for African American women is over 3 times that for White women.
- For every $1 a White man earns an African American man earns 74¢ and an African American woman earns 64¢.
- African American men represent 44% of the U.S. prison population.
- Homicide is the leading cause of death for African American men *and* women age 15–34 as opposed to third for White men and fourth for White women in the same age group.

[1] Sources for the following statistics are: Alan Guttmacher Institute; Centers for Disease Control; Children's Defense Fund; National Center for Health Statistics, National Vital Statistics System; National Urban League; The Sentencing Project; U.S. Census Bureau; U.S. Department of Labor, Bureau of Statistics.

- The official unemployment rate for African American men is over twice that for White men.

What does this portend for our lives? And our children and our young people, what are their chances for a good life?

- An African American baby has nearly 1 in 2 chances of being born poor. Expressed another way, nearly 45% of our children live in poverty.
- Our babies are over twice as likely as White babies to die in their first year of life.
- Our children account for 53% of U.S. pediatric AIDS cases.
- 25% of our children are being raised by high school dropouts.
- The teenage pregnancy rate among our girls age 15–19 is more than twice that of their White counterparts.
- The official unemployment rate for our youth is over 35% but when the hidden unemployment rate is factored in, the rate rises to about 60%.

Whenever the subject of the plight of the African American community is raised, the statistic invariably cited and highlighted as most problematic is:

*Nearly 44% of African American families
are headed by women.*

Indeed, the issue of female-headed households is central to many of the problems facing Black America. Its centrality, however, is usually misconstrued. For the implication or inference is often that these households are destined to fail because a woman is in charge. This is a red herring—and a sexist one at that.

The "problem" with these households is that more than half of them are poor. This means that these families are deprived of decent food, shelter, medical care, and education. Deprivation breeds frustration that can become so intense as to drive a mother to neglect or abuse her children, and propel a youngster into destructive and self-destructive behavior. When poverty reigns, no matter who is at the helm, the family members are at a greater risk of drowning.

The fact that economics—not gender—is at the heart of the matter becomes crystal clear when we look at an upper-income household headed by a single, divorced, or widowed African American woman. No one is terribly disturbed about such families because even though money does not guarantee Eden, it usually guarantees that the children will be decently fed, clothed, and housed. Money also means this woman can pay others to do the actual work of maintaining a household and she can afford to have "quality time" for herself and her children. Finally, on the issue of positive male role models, in a sense money can buy this, too, in the form of tutors and camp counselors, for example. In contrast, poor youngsters are often living in environments where they are exposed to a larger pool of negative as opposed to positive role models. And there is no way for them to buy out of this situation.

The statistic on female-headed households is a prime example of how statistics can be misinterpreted. To take another example, the high percentage of African American women who die in childbirth is clearly connected to, if not a direct result of, the fact that so few receive proper prenatal care. When we look at the disproportionate number of African American men incarcerated, we must remember that African American men are arrested more than their White counterparts and receive disproportionately higher rates of sentencing. Whenever statistics are used in a way that associates crime with African American men, we should not forget that most white-collar crime—which is not a victimless crime—is committed by White men. Given the poor quality of education and the infestation of crime and violence in some inner-city schools, is it any wonder that many of our young people drop out of school? Looking at statistics critically is not to deny the facts or absolve ourselves of all culpability, but rather it can give us a handle on the root causes of the problems so that we can deal with them more expediently and more humanely.

In view of the complexity of the problems that confront Black America, their solutions demand a multiplicity of approaches. In the 1960s a question often raised was, "Are you a nationalist or an integrationist?" In essence, should Black America be an island unto itself or a part of the nation. That was then, and is now, a false choice. We as a people have the right and responsibility to be fully included in American society, and an important dimension of this means being involved in national problem-solving initiatives. After all, the problems within the African American community are not exclusive to us. While we suffer disproportionately from such horrors as homelessness, AIDS, drugs, and teenage pregnancy, we are not the only people to know their sting.

How are we to address the devastating problems that haunt our communities? We have problems that make the charge that Black men are an endangered species more fact than rhetoric. We have problems that lead us to fear that a generation of our children has been lost. And we have problems that force us to say, on the eve of the twenty-first century, that the Black woman is still the victim of a triple jeopardy— discriminated against because she is Black, a woman, and usually poor. It seems so very clear to me that the deep and pervasive problems of Black America will not be solved by a "hands-off government," by a leadership that does not devote substantial sums of money and human resources to attack unemployment, poor health care, inadequate housing, and ineffectual education. The dependence on drugs and the rampant violence which stalk our communities are clearly in some ways related to the frustration and despair that result when people are without those social services really necessary to sustain a decent life.

But these are conservative times. These are days when poor folks are being asked to pull themselves up by nonexisting bootstraps, and folks of color are being told that protecting the rights of those who wish to discriminate takes precedence over any program of affirmative action. And yet we cannot give up. With a clarity of purpose we must vote for those national, state, and local candidates who demonstrate a serious commitment to addressing the needs of our children, our elderly, our poor. And with a clarity of purpose, we must continue to demand of our government that it care for *all* of the people all of the time.

At the same time that we look unashamedly to the government and the private sector for help, we must realize that the solutions to all our problems will not come exclusively from those quarters. We must roll up our sleeves and attempt to solve some of our own problems.

Self-help is not new to the African American community. Prior to integration (which for all its good definitely weakened some of our most valuable institutions), self-help was a way of life. Ironically, decades ago, during times of more overt and more brutal oppression than we now experience, we possessed a reservoir of values that enabled us to survive, and in many instances, thrive. There was a time when the stuff of Black values was ever before us, shoring us up. These values were reflected in our churches, our fraternal orders, our women's clubs, our sororities and fraternities, and other institutions through which African Americans shared what they had with other African Americans. Sometimes assistance came in the form of large individual donations, sometimes as the sum total of many small ones. A lot or a little, the money, the material goods, and the love behind them went a long way. In neighborhood after neighborhood it was African Americans who came to the rescue when an African American family was burned out of their home or the family's breadwinner was laid off.

These values were evidenced in our respect and care for our elders. But now, too many of the affluent among us have no time for the seniors, and the poor are slipping into deeper depths of poverty and so, have less and less for themselves let alone to share with anyone. In days gone by, women in our communities who did not work outside the home or who were retired watched over the young of their neighborhoods after school. These surrogate mothers offered a snack to tide the children over until dinner. They monitored their "gettin' to them lessons" and "stayin' outta trouble." But today, in many of our neighborhoods, elderly women live in fear that they will be attacked for what little their social security checks have given them, or disrespected if they dare to chastise or counsel the young.

We acted out these values in something as simple as the greeting, "How are you?" We used to really want to know how another was doing; and if the answer was, "Not so well," help was coming. Now we ask quickly and abruptly because we do not want to deal with the answer. We are often out of earshot by the time our neighbor says, "I am not doing so well."

When we look back at our early history in America, there were always government programs of assistance, but self-help was key to our survival. There were compassionate and "morally correct" White people, but in the main it was Black people who really cared about Black people. In our efforts to revisit and reinstill "ole fashion" Black values, the picture becomes hazy because there is so much of our history we cannot know. The very nature of our condition denies us a complete record. Despite the extant narratives we have on our lives in seventeenth-, eighteenth-, and nineteenth-century America, given the enormity of slavery, we have relatively few first-hand accounts. It is difficult, then, to know exactly how gracious, proud, resourceful, or disciplined we may have been, or indeed exactly how rebellious we were against the system. But there is one thing we do know: Simply to have survived bears witness to an extraordinary combination of virtues and abilities we have never been able to quite put together again. But we must! Of course it is pointless to indulge in woe-is-us-ism. As I once heard a brother say: "There will be no more prizes for predicting rain. It's time to build some arks!"

In recognizing that it is imperative that we do more for ourselves, we must also realize that the solutions to our problems are not to be found in the emergence of a hundred more sisters and brothers who secure top-level corporate positions. Such strategies, while important, are of the trickle-down nature. And we do not have the kind of time trickling takes.

It is important to recognize that many African American women, frustrated by reaching glass ceilings on their jobs or simply out of a desire to "be their own boss," are striking out into entrepreneurial activities. We can only applaud these initiatives when they are based on the kind of sound business principles that will allow them to keep the doors of their businesses open and their books in the black. But if such activity is only pursued for self-aggrandizement and our sister entrepreneurs turn away from the plight of others just as so many salaried women and men do, then our communities remain deeply in need.

For Black America to truly heal itself will require a kind of wholesale adoption: people adopting people.

This will entail a massive organization of ourselves for ourselves because the problem-solving cannot be left to lone-rider altruism. For example, 25 percent of our children are being raised by high school dropouts—many of whom are not even women, but girls. Their needs (mothers and children) cannot be successfully dealt with by saying, "Well, next Wednesday if I run into a sister who's a dropout and has a kid I might try to help her."

Some are quick to despair of any effective mobilization of our energies and resources because of the absence of a recognized national leader. This is not altogether a trivial concern. Those of us who came of age politically during the late 1950s and early 1960s, cannot help but think back to our most glorious moments under the leadership of Dr. Martin Luther King, Jr. We remember that whatever it was that we were doing, he helped us plug that into a national movement. While we may not have that now, we are not leaderless. Look around you, at African American assembly persons, children's rights advocates, presidents of block associations. Who are they if not leaders? As poet-essayist Nikki Giovanni pointed out in her essay "The Women's Alliance": "When people do not want to do what history requires, they say they have no 'role models.' "[2] To this I add: They also say they have no leaders.

We could always use more leaders: more congresswomen and men, school board officials, city councilwomen and men, trade union officers, mayors, governors, and even a United States President and Vice-President! But what we definitively must

[2] In *Sacred Cows . . . and Other Edibles* (New York: William Morrow, 1988).

have are "Sturdy Black Bridges,"[3] to connect us one to another, to make the reach tenable. With these bridges, as an Alice Walker poem urges, individuals can then, "Each one, pull one back into the sun." And in so doing, each becomes a leader, because leadership is first, foremost, and fundamentally service.

And what are these bridges? They are institutions and organizations created for, and in most cases by, African Americans. One that immediately comes to mind is, of course, the Black Church because we know that we literally would not have survived without it. Historically, it has been through the Church that we have cared for our sick, fed our poor, consoled our distraught—work which in a kinder, gentler nation would be a national responsibility. The reality, however, is that the Black Church is not and cannot be again the same institution that it was. The good work of individual churches notwithstanding, it is more difficult for the Black Church to play its historical role of full social-service agency, the primary reason being that today's problems are quantitatively and qualitatively more difficult to be addressed than in earlier times. For example, we have always had drugs in our communities, but never before have our children been so entangled in its web of death as both buyers and sellers. In the 1950s, V.D. was considered the scourge célèbre. But in no

[3] This term is taken from the anthology *Sturdy Black Bridges: Visions of Black Women in Literature* edited by Roseann P. Bell, Bettye J. Parker, and Beverly Guy-Sheftall (New York: Anchor Books/Doubleday, 1979). However, the ultimate source and inspiration is Carolyn Rodgers's poem "It Is Deep (don't never forget the bridge that you crossed over on)" in which she acknowledges her mother as her "sturdy Black bridge" (*How I Got Ovah* [New York: Anchor Press/Doubleday, 1976]).

way does it compare with AIDS. How do we deal with a modern-day plague of this magnitude?

Just because the complexity of problems has escalated beyond the traditional resources of the Black Church is not to say that it (like institutions of other faiths) is no longer a viable bridge, nor that it cannot become even more so. But if the Church is to serve as a major bridge over troubled Black waters, then even greater numbers of us must bring our energies, our creativity, our command of modern technologies and people skills to a most demanding mission: to feed the hungry, to clothe the naked, and to heal the sick. The Black Church may well be our most reliable bridge, but it cannot be our only one.

In our search for other bridges we do not have to start from scratch. We need to consider forging new building blocks, but much can be accomplished with the renovation of existing structures and greater attention to those that are already functioning well, such as the Children's Defense Fund; the National Black Women's Health Project; Hale House; the Southern Christian Leadership Conference; the National Association for the Advancement of Colored People; the National Political Congress of Black Women; the Association of Black Charities; the Urban League, the National Council of Negro Women, the Coalition of 100 Black Women and its sibling, the 100 Black Men. All around the nation there are scores of other organizations that provide on-site help, information, and referrals, and financial and material support for the needy. However, part of the reason many of these organizations are not as sturdy as they could be is that so few of us are aware of them. If these institutions and organizations had more hands, more people doing what only a few now accomplish, they would be all the more effective and all the more would get done. To put it bluntly, it means for you, my concerned sister, to wake up to the fact that in your city there are others already at work at the business of helping our people. You can join in.

It is *not* that difficult. It is *not* that complicated.

A sturdy bridge is, for example, a church with a program in which a large number of its members play dynamic roles in the lives of children in trouble and in jeopardy. Or, just imagine what it would be like if all our historically Black colleges and universities participated in adopt-a-class programs or after-school tutorial programs, and if our sororities and fraternities provided crews of volunteers for shelters for the homeless—volunteers able to attend to the crisis-needs of the homeless as well as equipped with information and training to assist these individuals as they struggle to enter a more productive life.

Clearly, such sturdy Black bridges will not arise from wishful thinking. The primary ingredients in fortifying our existing bridges and constructing new ones are time and money. And here we encounter a stumbling block.

Too many of us are not generous enough with our time, only we call it "too busy." But we all know that we find time for the people and pursuits that interest us. And thus, those who are truly interested in their people will find the time for them. Giving of your time can include serving as a mentor or support person for someone in recovery. Possibilities for more long-term commitments range from adopting to foster parenting to "big sistering" a youngster.

Those staunchly opposed to abortion might in particular consider putting their energies where their mouths are in terms of the sanctity of life by taking in a pregnant girl who sincerely wants to keep and raise her child but whose chances are slim if she must fend for herself and her yet unborn child alone. You can set miracles in motion by taking ten minutes to refer someone to a job training or adult literacy program or a counseling center. And if you're really feeling generous, in addition to the referral you might take the time to accompany the person there for the first time. If you are a proprietor of a business or someone with power when it comes to personnel, you can make good use of your time by purposely seeking out young African Americans to hire.

Not everyone is a one-on-one people person. And if you are not, but are serious about helping others, you can certainly volunteer as a support person for one of our bridges. If you have a skill—talking on the telephone, stuffing envelopes at top speed, processing data, writing, running errands—there is an organization that can use you well. Moreover, instead of summarily throwing out what you might call "junk," you can take the time to sort through what is good or salvageable and donate the items to organizations that can use them or that are in the business of distributing goods to the needy.

Time is truly one of our greatest resources and while it often translates into money, it is not a blanket substitute. Many who claim they cannot afford to make financial contributions could very well do so if they simply exercised a little restraint in one of the great American pastimes: Materialism.

We African Americans are Americans, and as such many of us are steeped in consumerism. We buy an extraordinary number of things, myself included. Take a look, for example, at the women on your campus, in your neighborhood, or in your workplace. Doesn't it take a long time before you see some of them wear the same outfit again? By acquiring more and more things, on some level we are straining to fill the need for certain nonmaterial experiences and emotions. We go out and buy yet another gadget, another item of clothing, another trinket, in hopes that it will fill a void in our lives, a void which is most likely a spiritual vacuum. Try as you might, you cannot fill that kind of void with things. But undaunted and in vain we persist. And sadly, after having just spent a hundred dollars on a "thing" with plans to do it again and again, when asked to respond financially to a needy person or a good cause, eyes roll, necks stiffen, heads turn, and fingers begin to fidget. Even more frightening, in many cases this selfishness is so deep that an individual is totally oblivious to it, and so, all the more brazen about it. Here I am reminded of a meeting where a pitch was made for a scholarship drive. A woman stood up and proudly proclaimed, "Well, I'll tell you what. You can have anything I didn't spend, because I just came from shopping." Without further ado and apparently feeling quite pleased with herself she then dropped two dollars in the basket.

For the sake of our future I think we must learn to give *before* we go shopping. We must also learn that giving can be simple and systematic. When you budget your money for food, shelter, clothing, and luxuries, include an item that allows you to contribute X amount of dollars per week, month, or year to help somebody or some institution that is working to help a lot of somebodies.

I certainly do not consider it a waste of time to encourage African Americans to give more of their time and money to the cause of sturdy Black bridges. It does, however, seem a little silly to provide an exhaustive list of the ways and means of doing it. As the suggestions above indicate, there is little I can offer that is novel or foreign to the African American community. I also know that when African Americans really want to do something, we are quite capable of figuring out the how. No doubt, as more of us embrace the concept of self-help, we will come up with all kinds of variations on the theme. Of course, following through on the tried-and-true methods and developing new ones will, to some extent, hinge on being inspired with right and righteous motivations.

What should motivate large numbers of African American women to become personally and consistently involved in helping their sisters and brothers is a combination of compassion and enlightened self-interest: compassion that flows from the understanding that there but for the grace of God and a set of circumstances beyond my control, go I; enlightened self-interest that realizes that people who are well-fed, well-housed, well-educated, and well on their way to leading productive lives are better and much safer people among whom to live. In short, if you are growing afraid of your own people, know that you, your children, and your grandchildren will spend your lives a hostage to fear if you do not *do* something.

As we build and refurbish our sturdy Black bridges, we must be mindful to conduct periodic reality checks on our motivations. For compassion and enlightened self-interest can easily dribble into superiority or voyeurism. That is to say, a bridge built on "Let us go over here and help the poor little underprivileged people" or "How could she have all those children?" is mighty shaky. That is paternalism *and* maternalism at its worst. If your eyes begin to drift off the prize, all you need do is remember the ties that bind. As an Australian aborigine woman put it: "If you have come to help me, then you are wasting your time, but if your liberation is bound to mine, then let us work together."

Far too many African American women are convinced that those who are several rungs below them on the socioeconomic ladder are there either by choice or by lack of will to climb any higher. An affluent woman and a crack-addicted woman may not at first glance seem to share much in common, but racism connects them. And so does sexism. The essential question is can either of them see a connection. It is not just can I, Johnnetta B. Cole, President of Spelman College, understand how I am bound to that sister who lives in a housing project a stone's throw away from campus, or up North in East Harlem, but does she see any relationship between herself and me. Admittedly, it is difficult to see yourself in others when their lives and circumstances are so different. When I see a photograph of a crack house it is difficult for me to see myself there, even as I focus on an African American woman who does not look that different from me. But just because it is difficult to make the connection, does not mean I cease trying. We both must work to see the connection and then, as the Australian aborigine woman said, "work together." Working together effectively will require finding common ground, not only in the big issues of life but in the everyday matters as well. I have the faith that African American women can do this. I truly believe that when two women sit down at a kitchen table, across a coffee table or a desk, they will be able to call on some common experiences. Some of it will center on men, some of it will focus on children and other deeply classic women's things such as keeping a household running. Finding common ground entails understanding that each can learn from the other. While it appears obvious what the affluent woman can offer the woman who lives a less privileged existence, there is a lot the latter can offer as well. We rarely acknowledge the extraordinary intelligence that many women exert in order to survive—be it recycling hand-me-down or well-worn clothing or feeding a family of four on what is essentially the makings of a dinner for two. We never use the word *intelligence* for such situations, but that is what it is. Making do when DON'T prevails is, quite simply, a kind of genius.

As we design new and reinforce old Black bridges, we must not overlook neighborhood organizations—which is, by the way, a level where things can really work without being smothered by bureaucracy. One drawback with the neighborhood model in the United States is that our neighborhoods are so class-bound; that is, those who need the most help are usually living among those who need the most help. Nonetheless, some very productive work can go on on the neighborhood level. For proof we need only look through the pages of the book *I Dream a World: Portraits of Black Women Who Changed America*. Here we meet tenant organizers, welfare rights advocates, organizers of domestic workers, who are women who have come from those very situations. Their accomplishments remind us that it would be the height of arrogance to assume that "the have-nots" are going to sit tight until "the haves" come to their rescue. In the case of initiatives that emerge from neighborhoods in distress, the role of the "outsiders" is not to usurp the leadership, but provide labor, ideas, money, and material that will facilitate the indigenous organizing.

The needy among us, we must also recognize, are not only women on public assistance, fixed incomes, and the working poor. Many African American women who ostensibly "have it all" are also in need of some sturdy Black bridges. Money and prominence can be great cover-ups, but they are not shields. Hence it is no secret that among the well-educated and well-off there are problems with substance abuse, physical and sexual abuse, suicide, and mental illness. And the middle-class and affluent Black woman is certainly not immune to experiencing loneliness, alienation, or confrontations with sexism and racism.

For these women, sturdy Black bridges already exist in our sororities and modern versions of early twentieth-century Negro women's clubs, such as The Links Inc. At the gatherings of such groups one finds a large percentage of women who can share with one another frustrations about being a single parent or what it means to be both an African American and a female in the corporate world. Just as within major professional disciplines there are women's caucuses and Black caucuses, hopefully we will soon see more Black women's caucuses as additional bridges of support.

Mary McLeod Bethune once admonished her sisters by saying that we Black women need to stop playing so much bridge and start building bridges. Indeed, we must by encouraging increasing numbers of African American women to pursue careers in science and engineering. But of course we must also build bridges that connect in sturdy ways the lives of those of us who have been blessed with skills, with education, and most of all with compassion with those among us stricken with poverty and despair. Sisters all, let us not underestimate ourselves and our power. Let us build sturdy, enduring Black bridges together. Let us find an organized way to love and to heal each other.

# She Who Learns
# Must Teach

*. . . for colored people to acquire learning in this country, makes tyrants quake and tremble on their sandy foundation.*
  —DAVID WALKER, *Walker's Appeal* (1819)

*Knowledge is the prime need of the hour.*
  —MARY McLEOD BETHUNE, "My Last Will and Testament," *Ebony* (August 1955)

EDUCATORS, activists, and assorted sages have given us scores of maxims that extol the value of education, but the most poignant words I have ever encountered on the necessity of education for African Americans were those of a Mississippi slaveowner who in 1832 wrote: "Knowledge and slavery are incompatible." Indeed, they are. And thus, it is not difficult to understand why at one point in American history it was illegal to teach slaves to read and write. Just as the denial of education is a proven method of subjugating a people, there can be little doubt that access to education is potentially a definitive means to the self-enlightenment and self-realization of a people, which in turn spells liberation. By that I mean liberation from all the "isms" previously discussed: racism, sexism, provincialism, and the individualism that prevents us from building sturdy Black bridges.

Some argue that nothing short of a violent revolution will end the poverty, racism, and sexism under which African American women live and labor. Violence may very well be a way of venting frustration, but in the long run it is not very constructive precisely because it provokes revenge and inevitably leads to more violence. As Dr. Martin Luther King, Jr., pointed out in *Stride Toward Freedom*, "The old law of an eye for an eye leaves everybody blind."[1]

There are those who reject violence and offer in-

[1] New York: Harper & Row, 1958.

stead the promise that more pulling of bootstraps will soon have the problem licked for African American women, no less than for African American men. Common sense, however, tells us that this is impossible if you have no boots because you are poor, or if you have had inadequate health care all your life and are too sick to pull the straps, or if you do not know what to do with bootstraps because you have not been properly educated about them.

There is also the view that patience will bring rewards, and we should just wait for matters to take their course. In Ethiopia there is a saying: "If you wait long enough even an egg will walk." But we hardly have that long to wait.

Clearly, there are many proposed strategies for the empowerment of African Americans, some of which have more viable and tenable features than others. But in the end, I always come back to education as the most consistent, obtainable, and, ultimately, most effective instrument for positive change. One reason people have problems with this concept is that it does not sound very glamorous, or quick enough; and we live in a society hooked on "the fabulous" and "the instant." No, education is not instant, but it can be life-changing. As tired and outraged as we may be about our predicament, we must remember that we did not arrive here overnight, and so, can hardly expect to escape it in the twinkling of an eye. Liberation is not a sudden event, but a process—a process I firmly believe will largely depend on another process called "education."

In advocating education as the most viable means of empowerment, I mean much more than our people's ability to read and write. I mean a process of intellectual development that should last as long as there is life within us. But, before any of this can even begin to happen one must be literate. While there may be reasons that there are illiterates among us, there is no excuse. Learning to read and write is no longer punishable by torture or death as it once was for slaves. Moreover, as imperfect a society as we live in, public libraries and educational programming on television are not among the services we lack. Obviously if you are reading this book, illiteracy is not among your problems. Then, why are you talking to me about illiteracy you might ask? Because we all need to wage a campaign against illiteracy in our communities and send a strong signal to our people that the inability to read and write among some of us is hazardous to our collective life. The more literate African Americans there are, the more of us there will be to engage in the process of education, empowerment, and liberation.

When I speak of education I do not mean formal schooling alone, nor the educational process as we have known it. Indeed, there is some validity to the argument that we have tried education and it didn't work. No, education as we have known it has not been a panacea, but at the same time this is in part because we have yet to "work" education to the fullest. Before we take a closer look at this issue, let us consider where we came from and acknowledge what we have gained from education as we have known it.

After Emancipation, African American women recognized that freedom had to mean more than the freedom to starve. They realized they would have to

work because African American males were often
unable to sustain a family on their incomes. Most
African Americans—men and women—advocated
the education of African American women for two
very practical reasons: first, better training and skills
were rewarded with better wages; and second, educated African American women could escape domestic service. Since the homes of Whites were places
where Black women were too often economically exploited and sexually assaulted, our foremothers
were eager to get out of those situations and Black
men were just as eager to have their womenfolk out
of domestic service. The ex-slave community is one
of the few where the education of females was frequently placed ahead of males. Often, African American men not only sacrificed their schooling, but also
undertook extra work so that a wife, sister, or
daughter could go to school.

In our historically Black colleges and universities
we have a legacy of a long and sustained effort by
African Americans for education. Each of our now
over one hundred such institutions was established
because African Americans were not welcome in
White colleges and universities. Despite their relatively meager resources, historically Black colleges
and universities provided African Americans with
virtually our only opportunity for higher education
and prepared us to compete in a hostile society.[2]

[2] Those who criticize historically Black colleges and universities as
segregationist would do well to note that these institutions have not
excluded those who are not of African descent. Long before predominately White schools were legally required to provide some semblance of
"equal access and opportunity," historically Black colleges and universities opened their doors to members of various racial and ethnic groups.

And in the face of this hostility and adversity, as time marched on, African Americans held fast to their faith in education.

As I grew up, there was all around me in the segregated Southern world of Jacksonville, Florida, a deep belief in the power of education, not only as a means for individual mobility, but as a key to our advancement as a people. Through what I was told and saw and through much that I experienced as a youngster, I first came to love and respect a process I later felt compelled to help others engage in. For as an African proverb tells us: "She who learns must teach."

The sacrifices African Americans have made for the sake of education are many and diverse, so much so that they have become part of our folklore. As I had been, many an African American child was sent North to live with friends and relatives, if parents thought the schools up there were better. Fathers and mothers cleaned somebody else's house, cooked somebody else's food, drove a car for lots of "Miss Daisies"—swallowing indignities that were bitter pills so that their children could get an education. "Why if Junior keeps doing as well as he's doing in school, one day he's going to be a doctor," proud parents would boast. "And Sister"—as the first girlchild in a family was often nicknamed—"Why Sister makes us just as proud as we can be," members of the extended family would proclaim. "Next thing you know she'll be done with school and be a teacher herself!"

---

Even today, taken as a group, these institutions' faculties and student bodies are more integrated than those at predominately White schools.

These snatches of conversation from my childhood resonate with the deep pride and high hopes parents and relatives had in the accomplishments of the next generation. To be sure, Junior and Sister would make more money than they did. But there was more at stake. There was also a sense that they would have more dignity, more power, and even, more joy.

There is much to be learned from what our folks say, and the way they say it. I recall an expression that was used in the South of my childhood and is still used today: "I ain't studin' you." That is what some said as an expression of disengagement, of ceasing to care, of deciding not even to bother to understand. Conversely, "Look how she studin' him," meant look how deeply she is trying to figure him out, to understand him. We were admonished to keep "studin'" our books because we were told "that's how you're gonna make somethin' outta yourself." And youngsters who didn't apply themselves in school heard the dire prediction: "He ain't never gonna amount to nothin'." For so many African Americans, along with cleanliness, studying and learning was next to godliness.

There was so much about segregated schools that was shameful and dehumanizing: using hand-me-down books White children no longer needed when they received brand new ones; being restricted to using the colored branch of the library which was never stocked with as good a collection of books as were found in the White branch; and, of course, there was little to no funding for extracurricular activities such as drama or band. But through it all many a Sister and many a Junior did go on to become something. Their education and educational setting may have been less than ideal, but the schooling they received prepared them for productive lives despite the constraints of a segregated society.

Of course we rejoiced in 1954 when in *Brown* v. *The Board of Education* the Supreme Court ruled that separate could not be equal, and segregated schools were struck down as unconstitutional and hence, illegal. Ironically, today in many public schools attended by African American youngsters, we find neither the strengths of the "colored schools," nor the advantages of a fully integrated public school system. In those "colored schools," more often than not there were African American teachers who believed in our children and their capacity to learn. With the so-called integrated schools, because of neighborhood segregation we often find African American students with White teachers, and many of our children are quickly and summarily labeled uneducable and left to fully *under*develop.

This is certainly not a plea for a return to the days of Jim Crow schools. But it is an urgent appeal for us to acknowledge and correct the realities of many of America's so-called integrated schools. Indeed, it is a plea for us to improve the state of African American education all the way up the academic ladder. Or to be more accurate, it is a call for us to pick up where we left off some thirty years ago on the issue of educational reform in America.

Following the assassination of Dr. Martin Luther King, Jr., and the urban rebellions in our cities, more and more predominately White colleges and universities opened their doors to more and more African Americans. The majority of these students did not come in and sit down quietly. Along with progressive professors and administrators, and fueled by the growing Black Power movement in their communities, these students launched the most serious critique ever raised about American education. In the sophisticated language of the academy, the charge was that from kindergarten through the post-baccalaureate level, American education was profoundly Eurocentric. In everyday language, it was called "racist," and labeled ineffectual for White as well as African American students. History classes introduced students to ancient Athens and Rome but never to the kingdoms of Mali, Songhai, and Ghana. When the great intellectuals of the Western World were discussed, instructors rarely came forth with the works of W.E.B. Du Bois or Frances E. W. Harper. Literature classes featured eminent writers such as Emily Dickinson, Joseph Conrad, and Ernest Hemingway, but never Margaret Walker, Chinua Achebe, or George Lamming. If the subject was music, students would be required to know about European classical music such as the masterpieces of Mozart, but Black classical music was ignored, denying students an encounter with the masterpieces of Coltrane. The economy of Europeans and their descendants would fill the curriculum, but few professors talked about West African work groups, Caribbean cooperatives, or African American quilting bees.

The Black Studies movement of the 1960s not only questioned *what* was being taught in American schools and colleges, it questioned *who* was doing the teaching, and demands were made for the hiring of more African American professors, to bring their perspectives and their voices to the table of scholarship. And, the Black Studies movement called for tearing down the walls that separated the academy from the community. It was argued that learning can and does take place outside of schoolhouses and universities, and that the sooner the theories of the academy came into closer communion with everyday community life, the better would be the process of education.

Those were incredibly turbulent and exciting times, and much good was accomplished. But the critique of American education put forth by Black Studies advocates remains valid today; and that critique itself became the subject of a fundamental criticism.

The very call for Puerto Rican Studies, Chicano Studies, Asian American Studies, Native American Studies, and Women's Studies represented a critique of Afro-American Studies. In short, Africans and African Americans had been inserted into a Eurocentric curriculum, but what of other peoples of color and very definitely, what of women? In calling for the inclusion of African and African American content and people in American education, Black Studies did not go all the way in terms of what an Afrocentric education should really mean. Perhaps this was a result of confusion about the meaning of the term "Afrocentric," a confusion still with us today.

It has always seemed to me that an African world view is definitively inclusive rather than exclusive. There is nothing about indigenous African and New World African-based cultures that rests on exclusivity. In fact, this has sometimes been to the detriment of Africa's people. For example, when the Europeans came with their particular form of Christianity, Africans simply incorporated it into their already expansive spiritual world. But then the time came when Africans would say: "When the Europeans came we had the land and they had the Bible, now we have the Bible and they have the land."

New World African-based cultures are certainly characterized by their incorporation of elements of different lifeways, such that throughout the Caribbean, Latin America, and indeed in parts of the United States, we can properly speak of a "Creole" culture, and *African American* ways of life. The point I want to make is that since an African world view is anything but exclusionary, an Afrocentric education would necessarily have to be one of inclusion. If by Afrocentric one means viewing the world from an African perspective which is, by its very nature, a view constructed from different cultures, religions, languages, and experiences, then let us promote it. However, if by Afrocentric education one means the study *only* of the world of Africa and the African diaspora, then that is dangerous because that is ethnocentric. To trade one ethnocentric education for another does not really help. In fact, it is a disservice to all. The truly well-educated person has a knowledge and a sensitivity about "self" as well as "others." She is familiar with her people's history, literature, art, politics, and economy, but she also knows about other human conditions that make up our world. Might we best then call for and promote a Worldcentric education? Clearly, it is a Worldcentric education that we African American women need if we are to be empowered.

Let me emphasize that my call for a Worldcentric

education is in no way meant to devalue Black Studies for African Americans. A conscious study of one's
self is as crucial for African Americans as self-exami-
nation is for people of other races and ethnic
groups. In fact, the empowerment of African American women requires an education in which our history and circumstances are acknowledged and ana-
lyzed, an education that *conditions* us to know
ourselves. People without a knowledge of who they
are cannot successfully participate in determining
the direction in which they wish to go.

There is great power in teaching young African
Americans about Thomas Jefferson, Thomas Paine,
and Abraham Lincoln but never of Ida B. Wells,
Anna Julia Cooper, and Mary Church Terrell. There
is great power in that act of *mis*-education because
the silence about African American women activists
suggests that we always have been, are now, and
must always be, no more than the recipients of what
is done to us and forever at the mercy of "the kind-
ness of strangers." Furthermore, a curriculum that
genuinely incorporated the complexities of African
American women's lives would, for example, reveal
that the reason there are only a handful of African
American women physicists is not because African
Americans are dumb and women can't do math!
Such an education would empower African American women because it would help us understand the
source of our powerlessness. Understanding is always the first step toward change. Again, as vital as
knowledge about self is, divorced from a genuine
understanding of other peoples' realities, such self-
discovery can promote insularity, provincialism,
and, indeed, ethnocentrism. That is why quite sim-

ply I ask, why not "Everyone's Studies"? Why not a full education where the world is center stage?

In my view, an education that produces people who know a lot but do so very little is hardly a true education. And thus, by Worldcentric I mean an education that not only teaches us about the world, but also *prepares* us to live purposefully in it. Such an education is structured, first and foremost, on the principle of social awareness and responsibility. This would mean that at the beginning of each lesson students would understand that the purpose of their education is to improve in some way the circumstances and conditions in the immediate and more distant world around them. The kinds and numbers of contributions an individual may make over a lifetime are limitless. Fundamental to this notion of awareness and responsibility is the idea that an individual must make some contribution—be it a single act of quantifiable and noticeable good, a stream of important but intangible good works that might well go unnoticed, or simply living in such a way as to do no harm.

When I say "awareness" and "responsibility" I do not mean noblesse oblige or elitist patronage, where individuals who feel guilty about having so much try to eradicate that guilt by performing deeds of little long-run consequence, such as offering food baskets to the poor at Thanksgiving time. Nor is it the social responsibility that emanates from pity, but rather the responsibility that emerges from a deeply instilled sense of community based on exchange and solidarity with others. This kind of responsibility develops only in an educational setting that insists on dialogue—cultural, intellectual, personal—within the rich diversity of humanity. Here we come to the second pillar of a Worldcentric education: knowledge of and respect for diversity.

An education grounded in a social responsibility for making the world a better place, hinges directly and completely on a deep, studied, and ongoing education about the complexities of human diversity and culture in all the neighborhoods of our nation, on all the continents of our world. This should include an education about those who can speak for themselves as well as those who historically have been voiceless and ignored. The histories of the poor and the powerless are as important as those of their conquerors, their colonizers, their kings and queens.

This multicultural, multipeople education should not, however, stop at academic knowledge about the human diversity of the world: an education in respect of that diversity must go hand in hand with learning about that diversity. This is, perhaps, the most difficult task of all, because throughout the ages people have been socialized to distrust and fear "the different." What's more, what should be a healthy sense of cultural pride gets distorted into chauvinism: the affirmation, "my culture, my ways are good for me" degenerates into the false conclusion that "my culture, my ways are the best for the entire world!"

Genuine respect for diversity can only develop in an educational experience that stresses there are no inherently superior or inferior ways of living, communicating, socializing, worshipping, working, or looking, and one that cautions students that a culture that pronounces itself as dominant can only live up to this "claim to fame" by dominating others. Education must prioritize in its curriculum and in its practice the multipatterned diversity within and outside our borders—which brings us to the third "pillar" of our Worldcentric education, which has to do with a new practice of education.

The place where learning takes place must change if the parameters of learning are to expand. Learning about the diversity of the world in such a way that respect and responsibility for that world is engendered, demands a restructuring of the environment in which knowledge about that world is acquired. No longer will libraries, lecture halls, and classrooms be sufficient. To these traditional venues must be added sites beyond the school grounds: that is, learning must go on in the very neighborhoods and communities of the cultures being studied. Students will have to learn from and with members of a community who may have never gone to school themselves. Students will have to learn in such a way that the experiences of those people are not only made real but learned in such a way that they will not be forgotten. This may mean living and interacting with those cultures and peoples that are different from the student's own; learning how to communicate, to understand, to share knowledge about history, culture, language, and living. All of this can only come about through a "participatory" education: participation by students in the lives of others. Only in this kind of educational environment can there emerge a genuine sense of social responsibility about the issues and struggles affecting the daily lives of diverse peoples.

Of course, students can engage in participatory

study and action in a community, but they may take on that educational journey such a preconceived set of myths and misconceptions about the host people that little if any learning or growth takes place. The assumption that a different way of life is ipso facto inferior to one's own is at the heart of an attitude anthropologists call "ethnocentrism," an attitude guaranteed to block education. From modern anthropology there are other important lessons to be learned about explorations, whether brief or sustained, into ways of life different from one's own. Over the past two decades, some anthropologists have urged their colleagues—and by extension any student—not only to study peoples in faraway, technologically underdeveloped societies, and the poor in their own society, but to engage in what anthropology professor Laura Nader called "studying up."[3] Coming to understand the culture of the elite in a society should be of no less worth and importance than understanding the masses.

Out of a new sense of responsibility will emerge a new concept of knowledge, a concept based on the acquisition of various knowledges rather than a singular one. Knowledge would then be based on the multiplicity of equally valuable truths instead of the dominance of one Truth. This new definition of knowledge would allow and encourage the investigation and analysis of everyone's lives, everyone's beliefs, everyone's struggles and dreams, so that no one ideological system could be understood as "science" while all others are called "superstition." All

[3] "Up the Anthropologist: Perspectives from Studying Up," in *Reinventing Anthropology*, edited by Dell Hymes (New York: Random House, 1972).

systems of thought would be appreciated for their coherence and rationality within their cultural context.

These pillars of a Worldcentric education—social awareness and responsibility, knowledge of and respect for human diversity, and participatory learning—would help create an environment in which creativity, imagination, and intellectual curiosity flourish. Each of these ongoing processes in our intellectual project would imbed in our communities of students the belief that all is possible, that each and every individual can have an effect, that each person can change and become an agent for others to change.

Such an education would also engender in people a zeal for lifelong learning: that insatiable curiosity about the world around you; that hunger to know more than you know; that outlook that says, "If that is the answer, then we better reexamine the question." Such lifelong learning means doubting not as a basis of incurable cynicism, but as a pathway to truths. This kind of education would train people to critically analyze and challenge established ideas rather than blindly accept what is written, said, or preached, to move beyond single and simple explanations and seek relationships and connectedness, and thus be better able to deal with contradictions and incongruencies.

Does it all seem terribly idealistic and out of touch with the real world? I suggest not. Ours is a world of incredible complexity, diversity, and change. From a very practical standpoint, simply to live in the real world today requires of us—as African American women, as American citizens, as citizens of the world

—a greater familiarity with different peoples and cultures. Economic relations and political events give a definitive ring of truth to the saying that our world is becoming smaller and smaller. Knowledge of other cultures, then, is not simply a frill or a pastime for people of leisure or an intellectual elite. It is essential knowledge for the business world which increasingly operates in an international context. Moreover, in our ever-so-rapidly changing world, many young people will change jobs several times during their adult lives. This kind of flux requires a flexibility and an openness to change for which a Worldcentric education will prepare them.

More importantly, however, my call for a Worldcentric education and lifelong learning is predicated on the conviction that the road to positive change, to addressing the severe problems which plague us as women, which plague our people, our country, and our world must involve actions by genuinely educated and concerned citizens. Only individuals properly educated about what life is really like for the poor of this planet will be able to help change their plight. Likewise, to put a freeze on the nuclear arms race, people must be truly educated about the dangers of a nuclear war and educated out of the xenophobia and warped sense of patriotism that often blinds us to the horror of what nuclear war would mean for the world community of human beings. As each one teaches another, we will come that much closer to increasing the numbers of citizens who will take the kinds of actions and exert the political pressure that will give us a chance to live in peace, with justice.

A Worldcentric education will certainly enable

people to deal with the problems that plague our society. For example, if you are in a setting where someone is talking in such a way that associates crime or being on public assistance exclusively with African Americans, then, my sister, you have to educate that individual right there. No, you are not in a classroom; no, you do not have books. But you have to have the knowledge and the confidence that knowledge brings to educate that person. The same principle applies in a situation where someone does or says something that is fundamentally sexist. One of the reasons we have been able to "afford" provincialism is because we have not been educated or self-educated to the rest of the world. Finally, if we consider the "Buppies" who distance themselves from their less privileged sisters and brothers, the problem is not necessarily that they don't know the condition in many African American communities, but that they have been educated not to care. The task then becomes to fully educate them about these conditions in a way that demonstrates definitively that no matter how far they have moved away from the "ghetto," as long as those conditions exist they are tied to them—if not in their own minds, then in the minds of White folks. Until they are educated to this connection they will not be able to make any real, sustained commitment to building those sturdy Black bridges that we need.

In some sense there is really nothing novel about this Worldcentric education I have outlined. It is simply an extended definition of what one dictionary says education is: "the act or process of imparting or acquiring general knowledge, developing the powers of reasoning, and generally preparing oneself or others intellectually for a mature life." To be sure, definitions of "mature life" may vary, but I hope you see my point.

Bringing true education down from the attic of theory and into our living rooms is an enormous undertaking, because it requires a restructuring of the very foundations and priorities of our educational system. Moreover, to uphold the basic tenets of a Worldcentric education is to implicitly and explicitly challenge some of the basic values of American society. It is here that the fundamental opposition to a Worldcentric education is found.

We live in a society that champions a kind of rabid individualism, which manifests itself in the acquisition of individual achievement and wealth to the exclusion and often at the expense of the good of the community. So ingrained is this "ism" that in the late 1980s a record 76 percent of college freshmen identified being well-off financially as a key goal of getting a college education. We live in a society where tolerance, not to mention respect for differences, is particularly low. In so many places—from corporate board rooms to suburban classrooms to neighborhood pool rooms—the message and the sentiment is: All people of color are in the category of "other" in relationship to White Americans; the proper place for women is in the house; heterosexuality is the only normal way; the poor are that way either because they prefer it to being "normal" (that is, middle and upper class) or their plight is, for a host of reasons, their own fault. On the international scene there is a chauvinism which argues not only that our system is the best for Americans, but that it is the best and only system that any nation should have.

In contrast, Worldcentrism fully acknowledges and respects the multicultural, multiethnic, and multinational character of America as well as the world. Worldcentrism puts the interest of the community over that of the individual. And Worldcentrism disallows *any* ideology of inherent superiority or inferiority.

Clearly, the issue of educational reform is a multifaceted thing, and the issues within the issue are numerous and complex. They include the question of choice (students and their parents choosing where they will go to primary and secondary school); the role of national tests in setting a common curriculum; the degree to which curricula are multicultural; and still—in the 1990s!—the question of busing to achieve racial integration. The outcome of these and other debates will determine in large measure the very nature of America in the coming century. Needless to say, as America goes, so goes Africa America.

These are the issues confronting us, sisters. We can choose to disengage ourselves from the struggle, we can choose to limit, simplify, and thus ignore the issues, or we can meet the challenge head-on, in all its complexity, in all its demands, and in all its potential for change—change that would truly be for the betterment of African Americans, our society as a whole, and the world at large.

It is easy to talk about what is wrong with American education in general and certainly about the deplorable state of education for large numbers of African Americans. Reports abound on high school dropout rates, the profusion of drugs in our schools, the greater number of college-age Black men involved in the criminal justice system than in attending colleges and universities, the paucity of minorities and women in the sciences, the inability of large numbers of American students to demonstrate basic competence in reading and mathematics.

So serious are the problems in our schools that the early 1990s have seen the President of the United States, Governors, and even local officials identify addressing these problems as a cornerstone of their administrations. Never before have we had a self-appointed Education President and Education Governors. And never before have we seen the corporate world participate so actively in school-reform projects. Such involvement is motivated by a concern that a poorly educated America will not be able to compete in a world where the workers of other nations know more and produce more than American workers.

There is good reason for the concern of the business world, government officials, and educators themselves over the state of education in America. And thus new programs, reforms, and specific suggestions for change abound. I, too, wish to offer some lessons for improved education, but I do so based on the proven record of success at a Black women's college called Spelman.

What is the secret of the Spelman success story? What lessons can we learn for Black education today, indeed for the education of all in America from kindergarten on up the educational ladder?

**1.** Spelman women have their basic necessities cared for, live in a relatively safe environment, and are not haunted on campus by racism and sexism, and as a result can turn their attention to their studies. **Lesson:** Education involves the whole person. It is hard to teach hungry, abused, scared, or oppressed children or adults.

**2.** The women and men of the Spelman faculty are seriously committed to the education of these young women. **Lesson:** A good teacher is central in the learning process. Students will soar when teachers bring to the classroom a passion for their discipline and a concern for the well-being of their students.

**3.** At Spelman, students see individuals who look like them serving as the president of the college, a professor of biology or economics, the president of the student body, editor of the newspaper, and captain of the basketball team. **Lesson:** Positive role models encourage high self-esteem, which is a necessary ingredient for learning. Positive role models boost a student's pride and sense of self-worth.

**4.** At Spelman there is no assumption that Black folks don't like math and women cannot do science (37 percent of Spelman students major in mathematics, the sciences, computer science, and a dual degree program in engineering). There is no assumption that women are just not as bright as men and will never understand economics as easily as men do. On the contrary, the assumption is that Spelman women will excel in all of their studies . . . and they do. **Lesson:** High teacher expectation is important to learning. Teacher expectation brings student success.

**5.** Spelman women are required to take a course in African American Studies or Women's Studies before they graduate. But, perhaps more importantly, the realities of African Americans and women are mainstreamed into the entire curriculum. **Lesson:** The content of the curriculum should never exclude the realities of the very students who must intellectually wrestle with it. When students study all worlds except their own, they are miseducated.

**6.** It is as if a family, indeed a community comes to Spelman behind each student. **Lesson:** The involvement of parents or surrogate parents in the education of their children is a crucial element for student success. Knowing that there are individuals who care about their welfare and educational progress is an incentive for students to excel.

If I had to summarize the lessons the Spelman experience has taught me about the education of Black folks, it would be this: In an atmosphere relatively free of racism and sexism, where teachers care and expect the very best, parents and kinfolks are involved, and the curriculum and those around the students reflect in positive ways who the students are —there are no limits to what individuals can learn and who they can become.

My sisters, the time has come to take an even closer look at the role of education in the empowerment of African American women, realizing that when we are empowered so, too, will be all African Americans. Although the logic behind this is obvious, it bears repeating: Women are the primary caretakers of children and, consequently, their first teachers. So, as they say, when you educate a man you educate an individual, but when you educate a woman, you educate a nation. This is why we must learn, and we must teach. If we need role models we can certainly look to our foremothers.

Remember that nameless West African woman who represented all our foremothers. Despite grueling work and ignominious abuse she became both a student and a teacher. She recognized her powerlessness and set out to explore paths back to empowerment. First she taught herself a new language. It certainly was not the standard American English of the time, but it was at least enough to communicate with her slavekeepers and fellow slaves. And in this her motives were quite simple: Language would at least give her the power to name things in her captors' own words. This woman studied "White folks' ways," not in any grotesque desire to emulate them, but in order to recognize and anticipate the many faces of oppression, brutality, and cruelty.

One of the most invaluable contributions this woman made to her community was in her efforts to train her children. By passing her knowledge on, she expressed a willingness to embrace the future and a strong unwillingness to accept her horrible condition as hopeless and unchangeable. This woman was a teacher. It is wonderfully romantic to think she consciously and actively taught her children African history and culture, but such was neither practical nor reasonable. Her lessons were much more basic, much more survival-oriented. This woman taught important life-and-death lessons. She taught her children to be alert when Whites were present and to study their faces just as she did. She taught them to plant codes in the songs they sang and secret gardens in the woods. She gave swift, practical lessons, designed to impart information. She stole snatches of formal education from the slaveholder's children. But formal education was not at the core of the African woman's teachings. She taught what we still refer to as Mother Wit. In slave-quarter churches and secret, forbidden meetings she preached the principles of survival and such survival tools as herbal medicine and North Star navigation. She taught the art of endurance and the beginning of resistance.

This nameless West African woman who survived the middle passage, who lived in spite of slavery, somehow found the courage and the righteous indignation to struggle for a future she knew she would never see. She chose to endure and determined in her mind not to surrender, but for her own sake and the sake of generations to follow, to keep her will and her soul alive. This nameless West African woman is a giant on whose shoulders all of us stand.

# In Closing...?

ON THE AVERAGE, books have conclusions that do one of three things. Most often, they repeat what has already been said. For me to do this would be an insult to my very intelligent sisters because, quite frankly, whatever you did not "get" is either not worth repeating or perhaps just not for you; and whatever you "got" you are more than capable of keeping without any reminders from me. Another conclusionary tactic (for even those books solidly grounded in reality) is to take off for pie in the sky, to leave readers with an easy, foolproof-sounding plan of action, such as do thus and such and you, too, can lose fifteen pounds in a week, become a millionaire in nine months, or turn your life around one, two, three. Such conclusions, for all their good intentions and feel-good appeal, are simply out of touch with the day-to-day realities of people's lives. Lastly, many books end too definitively in a closure mode, that in effect says, "There, you have it. End of discussion." Clearly that is inappropriate here because this has been, after all, a conversation; and I don't want us to stop talking. It is, in fact, now your turn to talk (and yes, even talk back!). And so, I invite each of you, my sisters, to write your own conclusion to this book. If you find this the least bit intriguing, then you might want to mull over the following suggestions.

For starters, consider writing your memoirs—in miniature, or the whole nine yards—keeping in mind that ideally you want to tell your story within the larger context of *her*story. If you think that this is a frivolous or self-indulgent thing to do, believe me, it can be a very insightful, cleansing, cathartic exercise. You will invariably relive some forgotten joys, as well as confront, and perhaps make peace with, some painful, even traumatic experiences. The destination point of this journey is, of course, Yourself: who you are as an African American, as a woman, as a human being; who you don't want to be, who you want to keep on being, who you wish to become. I might add that if you are not up to an in-depth, analytical review of your life, know that even a simple, straightforward chronicle of your life is a worthy undertaking. It will provide you with a very tangible something to pass on to the younger generation of your family and friends to help ensure that the circle will, indeed, be unbroken.

Whether or not you actually write out your life's story, after taking a long look at your life, imagine that you've just become President of the United States. Now, my sister, what *are* you going to do about racism and sexism? What policies would you promote? What programs would you initiate? For example, recognizing that our nation has historically carried out a policy of affirmative action for White Anglo-Saxon men, would you support affirmative action for the rest of the populace?

I remember enjoying a Soul Quotient Test. In the 1960s, it was a fun way to make the point that familiarity with African American culture was not evenly distributed among people, including Black folks. As a part of your conclusion to this book you might develop a Provincialism Quotient Test with items such as:

- If asked to complete the statement "Black women are located in the following countries":, how would I fill in the blank?
- Did I assume that because it has nothing to do with me, I let news on the S & L crisis go in one ear and out the other?
- Have I ever really read the Constitution of the United States?
- In conversation have I overheard myself saying things like, "Oh, she's Chinese or Japanese, what difference does it make"?
- Do I know the difference between Spanish and Hispanic? Do I care?
- When I pass a movie theater showing a foreign film, do I automatically think, "Oh, that's not for me"?
- How many activities have I refrained from because I felt they weren't the "Black thing" to do?
- If a map of Africa were put before me, how long is it going to take me to locate Mali?

If you agree that there is a need for more African American women to become engaged in building "sturdy Black bridges," do a little brainstorming as to what your next community-service involvement might be. If after a few minutes you find yourself up against a blank piece of paper, then one way to approach it might be to ask yourself what particular issue or issues are you concerned about. Is it homelessness? Rape? Education? Substance abuse? Then consider what you can reasonably and consistently do about your concern. If you are already involved in building sturdy Black bridges, outline a plan of action that would entice and convince more of your sisters to join in the construction project. By the same token, if you feel that more self-help is either not in order, or should be way down on the list of priorities, then identify and expound on what you think should be the first order of business in terms of addressing the problems that confront our Black communities.

Finally, my sisters, review your formal educational experience from kindergarten to as far as you have carried it out. Ask yourself how well it has served you in life. Make a list of what went right and what went wrong. Then, based on that list, discuss how you would change education for African American women in a way that would make a whole lot more go right than wrong.

I realize it is quite possible that not a single one of the "passages" I have suggested you write suits your style or your fancy. If so, that is quite all right. I just want to encourage you to write your own conclusion to this book—even if it is nowhere else than in the privacy of your mind. But most of all, my sisters, let's keep talking.

## About the Author

Johnnetta B. Cole graduated from Oberlin College and later earned an M.A. and Ph.D. in Anthropology from Northwestern University. She is the author of two anthropology textbooks which are used in classrooms throughout the United States. Prior to assuming the presidency of Spelman in 1987, Dr. Cole held positions at Washington State University, the University of Massachusetts at Amherst, Hunter College, and the City University of New York. She is married to Arthur J. Robinson, Jr. and is the mother of three sons and two stepsons.